AUGUSTIN-MICHEL LEMONNIER

presents

# L I G H T
## OVER THE SCAFFOLD
Prison Letters of Jacques Fesch

and

# C E L L   1 8
Unedited Letters of Jacques Fesch

*Guillotined on October 1, 1957 at the age of 27*

Preface by Michel Quoist

Translated by Sr. Mary Thomas Noble, OP

ALBA · HOUSE    NEW · YORK

SOCIETY OF ST. PAUL, 2187 VICTORY BLVD., STATEN ISLAND, NEW YORK 10314

Originally published in French under the title *Lumière sur l'échafaud*,
© Les Editions de l'Atelier, Paris, 1972.


Library of Congress Cataloging-in-Publication Data

Fesch, Jacques.
    [Lumière sur l'éschafaud. English]
    Augustin-Michel Lemonnier presents Light over the scaffold:
prison letters of Jacques Fesch, guillotined on October 1, 1957 at
the age of 27 / translated by Mary Thomas Noble.
        p.     cm.
    Translation of: Lumière sur l'éschafaud and of Cellule 18.
    Title on added t p · Augustin-Michel Lemonnier presents Cell 18.
    ISBN 0-8189-0750-9
    1. Prisoners — France — Religious life.  I. Lemonnier, Augustin
-Michel.  II. Fesch, Jaques. Cellule 18. English.  III. Title:
Cell 18.
    HV9667.F4813     1996
    282'.092 — dc20                 96-1520
    [B]                               CIP


Produced and designed in the United States of America by the
Fathers and Brothers of the Society of St. Paul,
2187 Victory Boulevard, Staten Island, New York 10314,
as part of their communications apostolate.


ISBN: 0-8189-0750-9

**Printing Information:**

Current Printing - first digit   1   2   3   4   5   6   7   8   9   10

Year of Current Printing - first year shown

1996      1997      1998      1999      2000      2001

# LIGHT OVER THE SCAFFOLD

and

# CELL 18

.

# CONTENTS

# L I G H T
## OVER THE SCAFFOLD
Prison Letters of Jacques Fesch

This work combines two books previously published separately, containing the letters of Jacques Fesch: *Light Over the Scaffold* and *Cell 18*.

Some revisions have been made, notably in *Light Over the Scaffold*, in order to restore certain letters to their chronological order.

On the other hand, in order to present a more complete picture of the personality of Jacques Fesch, we have inserted, in the correspondence with Brother Thomas in the first book, some extracts from letters which Jacques had written on the same dates to Madame Polack.

The reader will therefore not be surprised to find these same passages again in their proper context in *Cell 18*.

# PREFACE

This is an absolutely extraordinary document. First, because it is highly unusual, and with good reason, to have the letters of someone condemned to death, and second because the spiritual richness of these texts has reached a degree rarely equaled.

I join Augustin-Michel Lemonnier in thanking Madame Fesch for having allowed us to publish this astounding testimony.

I take the liberty to assure Mademoiselle Fesch, the "little Veronica" of the letters, who is now grown-up, that she should never be ashamed of her father. On the contrary, she should read these letters with pride. This mysterious father whom she no longer remembers has left her a terrifying but beautiful witness. Jacques Fesch had the courage to resist the most atrocious temptation of all, that of despair. His witness is that of a man who believed in the unconquerable strength of a God who is Love, whose love no crime can overpower, and which is stronger than death itself, even the most horrible death.

Dear Madame Fesch, dear Veronica, I am convinced that your husband, your father, is close to the Lord. He now offers you, if you are willing to accept it, something he could never give you in this world: a love wholly new, regenerated and transfigured by the very love of the Crucified One.

And to you who will take this book in hand, I would say: You will probably race through it. You will want to know how Jacques died. If you do dash ahead like this, I beg you to go back afterwards, and reread some of the letters very quietly, at your leisure. If not, you will be missing some very real treasures. Jacques was gifted. Briefly, often in a few words or phrases, he was able to describe some fruit gathered along the path of his soul's journey or to convey an exceptional spiritual experience. If you know how to pause, meditate, and pray as you read, you will discover more clearly here than you might in learned treatises that Jesus Christ is present in the hearts of those who suffer. You will realize that no matter what our failings may be, He is always ready to take possession of us, liberating us, and pouring into our souls His infinite joy. You will come to see that every life calls for reverence, and that, regardless of how it appears to the human eye, if only it is open to love it cannot fail to be a redeeming power for all of humanity.

In Jacques Fesch's letters, no attempt has been made to disguise names and places. I am happy to make these letters available to the general public, and I am convinced that they will bring many to an encounter with the one Savior. I pray for all who may read them.

Through Jesus Crucified, I beg Jacques, who was guillotined,
to teach us how to carry the burden of our sins,
to teach us how to suffer,
to teach us how to die.

*Michel Quoist*

# CHAPTER 1

# THE TRAGEDY

On February 26, 1954, the French press circulated the following news release:

> Last Thursday, a little before six in the evening, Alexander Silberstein, a money-changer, was attacked in his shop at 39 rue Vivienne, in the Paris stock exchange. He bled copiously while his attacker, Jacques Fesch, carrying a large amount of money he had just stolen from him, fled down the street with passersby in full pursuit.
>
> A policeman, George Vergnes, who had just been alerted, chased the thief as far as the Boulevard des Italiens, where Fesch disappeared into the building at No. 9. A little later Vergnes saw Fesch crossing the courtyard, and when he issued the usual warnings the latter responded by firing on him. Vergnes fell, mortally wounded. The author of this crime, a well-dressed juvenile delinquent, was only caught finally at the exit of the Richelieu-Drouot subway, thanks to the cool expertise of a former inspector of the Criminal Investigation Department: Marcel Redier.

The man who was to be jailed and condemned to death on the guillotine had committed his double crime for the sake of a castle in the air — a dream he had of buying a boat in which he might escape from his life situation.

But let us return to the drama and study the details as they unt>or> 6 LightR THE SCAFFOLD

folded. First of all we must know that Fesch, in order to succeed in his assault, had gone to his father's house in the province, and unknown to him had looked for a revolver with which to attack Silberstein. The gun was loaded. He removed the bullets, and did not put them back until he was with R., his accomplice, and ready to set out for the attack. In addition to this he provided himself with a hammer. It would be useless to pretend there was no definite premeditation in all this.

He had first gone to Silberstein's place during the day to order some money, then returned in the evening presumably for the remainder of the cash, as if he had only received a part before. Taking advantage of the money-changer's preoccupation, Fesch struck him with the butt of his revolver, stunning him. But the old man, streaming with blood, called for help. Fesch fled, but in striking his victim, the trigger of his revolver had been released, and a bullet shot out, wounding Fesch's hand as it went. He too was therefore bleeding, and this drew the attention of the people in the street. Followed by the crowd, he came to the rue Saint-Marc and arrived at the Boulevard des Italiens. Seeing a building with an open courtyard he dashed in, but in his mad race dropped his handkerchief. In spite of the pursuers close on his heels, he stooped to pick it up. Then he ran up the stairway to the top of the building. They lost his trail. He was on the fifth floor. He waited there until things should "quiet down." Then, to allay suspicion, he went down again "very calmly" as if nothing had happened. He reached the courtyard only to find that the street entrance had been blocked off. A group of pursuers and a police agent were waiting there. Fesch acted as if he did not know any of them, and they seemed not to recognize him. He was about to make his exit when someone recognized him and cried out, "There he is!" The policeman shouted, "Hands up!" Fesch turned around immediately. Seized with panic, he drew forth his wounded hand which he had kept concealed in his overcoat pocket, and fired a single shot straight through the policeman's heart. He then drew the bolt of the main door opening into the street and dashed out, followed by the shouts of the crowd that had gathered there. A man by the name of Lenoir tried to seize him. Fesch took aim and shot a bullet which, instead of severing the man's spinal cord, fortunately slipped along the vertebral column. Nevertheless the man was seriously wounded. Fesch made a dash for the Richelieu-Drouot subway station. Two people again attempted to stop him, one of them a former police inspector. Fesch fired twice at them, but missed. He was finally caught in the subway station.

This is the story in all its authentic detail — a lurid "Western". It explains to some extent the pitiless reaction of the jury at the time of the trial.

Yet it is important to consider objectively who this man was, and what the reason was for his criminal actions.

# CHAPTER 2

# WHO WAS JACQUES FESCH?

Upon his arrest Jacques Fesch was subjected to the usual police interrogation and then taken without delay to the Prison de la Santé in Paris. A half hour later the prison chaplain entered his cell. He found a man in a state of collapse, who told him he had no faith and politely dismissed him. The chaplain did not insist. He knew there would be plenty of time to visit again.

The child of Belgian parents, Jacques Fesch was born in Saint-Germain-en-Laye, on April 6, 1930. His father, a bank president, was autocratic by nature and made family life unbearable. He paid little or no attention to his son, save for a systematic attempt to destroy in the child all his enthusiasm, confidence, optimism, and faith. The boy was loveable, however, and had a genuine affection for his mother.

For nine years Jacques attended a religious school in Saint-Germain-en-Laye, but family problems at home had robbed him of a sense of security and enthusiasm, and as a result he did poorly in his studies. Next he was enrolled in a boys' high school. After spending one year there, he definitively gave up all study. He was eighteen.

His father tried giving him a job in the bank. Jacques showed little interest in this, but did continue with the work until his departure for military service. Toward the end of his military service his parents, who were living in a large house in Saint-Germain-en-Laye, separated. His father withdrew to Anjou while his mother took a small apartment in Saint-Germain-en-Laye.

In appearance Jacques was tall and slender, with an oval face and fine features. He had a nonchalant air about him and always seemed a bit absent-minded. This is how his lawyer described him: "He always looked as if he needed a shot in the arm, so pronounced was his apathy."

At twenty-one, during his military service in Germany, he married Pierrette Polack, a young girl of Saint-Germain. At home a little girl, Veronica, was born. After Jacques' return from service his father-in-law gave him a job in his company in Strasbourg. Eventually a conflict arose. We have to admit that in the dispute, Jacques did not play a very admirable role. Jacques and Pierrette, not mature enough for married life, had soon separated — the crime took place a few months after this separation — and Jacques returned to live with his mother, while Pierrette went home to her parents with Veronica in October of 1953.

Jacques had the idea of founding a branch office of his father-in-law's business, a thermal coal company. Madame Fesch, his mother, gave him a thousand francs toward this project, half of which he promptly spent on a car. He soon realized the impossibility of carrying out his plan, or of justifying his use of the money his mother had given him.

Discouragement gradually settled in Jacques' soul and became habitual. He turned to easy solutions. Longing to escape from all that made up his dismal life, he dreamed of setting sail for Polynesia in a small boat. He was thoroughly disillusioned by an existence without ideals and keenly conscious of being a total failure. Plagued with the feeling that everything had gone wrong for him, he clutched at a single straw: to salvage his situation by a voyage to distant lands. In the meantime he returned to his wife, "taking refuge with her" as she was to say.

Then Jacques left for La Rochelle. There he had plans for a sailboat drawn up, small but sea-worthy. His dream was on the point of coming true. But he was short two thousand francs of the cost of the boat's construction. His father refused to help. Jacques was determined to leave all the same, cost what it might — to get away from this miserable life that he and his family were leading in their different ways. It was stifling him, and the thought soon became an obsession. He could think of nothing else. What had started as a dream was now a fixed idea, leading up almost inevitably to the tragedy.

He laid his plans with two friends, delinquents like himself, weak accomplices who did not stand by him to the end and were acquitted at the trial.

Here you have the roots of the tragic story of this total misfit.

Misfit? That is easy to say, judging from the world's point of view. Easy to say, true, but the reality was far more complex. Someone who knew Jacques Fesch had this to say about him, at the first unfolding of the drama:

"My daughter-in-law knew Jacques well. They were friends from childhood. He was a delightful boy, reserved, a little withdrawn, but very sweet. She wonders how on earth all this happened."

"What about his parents — did you know them?"

"Frightful parents! The father was both spineless and cynical. The mother, weak. It's just one more instance of the child paying for the sins of the adults."

# CHAPTER 3

# JACQUES AS SEEN BY PIERRETTE

On the evening of the blood-drenched day when her husband became a criminal, Pierrette was waiting to meet him in a cafe in the capital. But it was the police who met her instead. With scant ceremony, and no explanation, they ordered her to follow them. Then suddenly, two feet in front of her, she saw her husband, handcuffed, his face bleeding. (We can surmise the cause of his wounds.)

Pierrette was given the third degree. They questioned her from eight that evening until three in the morning, without ever telling her the reason for her detention. Incredible, isn't it?

On the afternoon of the next day, on being handed over to another agent, one at last who was human, Pierrette asked for a newspaper. The headlines shrieked that her husband was an assassin.

When the stampede of photographers began, this agent once more had pity on her. He covered her with his cape, to hide the suffering in her face.

Madame Marcelle Auclair, who knew Pierrette Fesch well, wrote about her: "Not for a moment did she disassociate herself from her husband. She was a faithful wife, so simple, so upright, so courageous."

And these are Pierrette's words:

Our life was difficult, but we understood each other perfectly. And when Jacques came home from the army, he set to work with a will. He was interested in coal from the point of view of mineralogy (my father's company, where Jacques was working, was a coal corporation). But then the question of anti-Semitism came up.[1] There were altercations; things went from bad to worse... What could Jacques do? Our parents were furious with us. I was helpless.

> Pierrette forgave, forgave so completely that she told her
> little Veronica that her papa was away on a trip.

If I had believed that her father was a good-for-nothing, I would have been a criminal to teach my little girl to love him... Jacques is not bad. His natural disposition is good. If he never knew the difference between good and evil, it was because no one ever helped him to understand this. He relied solely on himself from his fourteenth year on. In that one year he grew twelve inches... This was a time when he needed someone to be concerned about him, to take care of him. But he was left to his own resources. His mother was very unhappy, his parents were separated. His father was lost in cosmic considerations: "A human life, that's a small thing... What is a woman? A plaything..." His father carries a very heavy weight of responsibility.

My little Veronica is very sweet, very sensitive, and like her father, very withdrawn. Seeing her, I can picture what Jacques must have been like as a child. Perhaps he came to me to escape from the world in which he was living. He was passionately interested in travel, geography, mineralogy. It is not true that he was an idler. I have seen him tackle work relentlessly. There was in him a keenness for research which would have been very constructive if it had been directed. He always tried to overcome obstacles, even though they were sometimes enormous. The idea that he dodged all effort is wrong.

Jacques was an upright boy. In all his twenty-seven years, he was never involved in anything suspect or shady except during the

---

[1] Pierrette Fesch had some Jewish blood in her.

two months which preceded his act of folly. You would have said that he was sinking deeper and deeper into discouragement, trying to disappear. He always bore within himself a sense of failure. He could not go on... As for me, I sensed that something fatal was hanging over our heads. Things were not the same any more. When he came back to me for refuge, trying to set up our life together once more, he talked of nothing but the boat... I thought he was trying to conceal some escapade from me. Up till then, he had always been a faithful husband... I could not foresee that his obsession about the boat was to end in tragedy.

Since the verdict, what has struck me is his extraordinary simplicity. He didn't think he could possibly be condemned, and yet he accepted it. He simply said, "I hope they won't carry it out to the finish..." He sent me tender, moving letters, and then suddenly he would write something humorous: "I walk like a teddy bear in chains..." I would weep at the beginning of a letter, then laugh in the middle. And this became disconcerting. For example, he ended one serious, reflective letter with: "Just the same, Veronica has a rascal for a father." Another time, he wrote to me, "I am glad that Veronica has a happy face and welcomes you with flowers. Does she sometimes talk about her papa, whom she used to wait for so impatiently at noon?... She was so sweet and nice. But what can you expect? At twenty, one is not a father. Some never are at any age..."

About his mother, he wrote:

She is a mother by instinct, I might even say, animal instinct. She would do anything for her children, but doesn't know how to go about it very well. She cannot understand other people, and still less can she make herself understood. She never communicates with a person's soul, because she is too reserved... There was always a great deal of constraint in our relationship, due to this lack of intimate contact... She is a perfect mother for very small children, simply because all they need is attention and smiles...

To Pierrette, he wrote:

Poor treasure, I never spoiled you very much. Do you know what I would like to do? I would like to be able to offer you what would have given you the most pleasure: an antique silver bracelet which you could always wear on your wrist. But here, this is a little difficult to manage. I promise, though, that as soon as it is possible, I will make you a present of this. Alright? My love, don't be sad, not ever, and don't give up hope. I love you very much, and I'll prove it to you. . .

# CHAPTER 4

# JACQUES' EXPLANATION

Jacques Fesch, murderer, is in prison. Under maximum security. Alone, confined within four walls. In his soul it is night. His dream of escape upon the high seas has evaporated into thin air. As for the rest of the world, life goes on.

The man has committed murder. In total isolation, he considers through long hours the negative consequences of his rebellion and crimes. He does it without self-indulgence: "I have done much evil." He does it with no less indulgence for the circumstances of his life. Soberly, drily even, but without rancor, he ponders. Finally, in a report which he wrote at the request of the prison chaplain, he expresses himself, not as a journalist certainly, but with the sincerity of a defeated actor at the end of a tragedy which is his own. His lucidity is remarkable. Reading the text, we begin to understand the psychology of a condemned man.

My impressions are contradictory, and it is hard to put them into words. Obviously, the exceptional situation in which I find myself has colored and modified my character in a more or less visible and discernable way, so that a significance is attached to each event, and a light thrown on it, that is quite certainly false. Again, unconsciously, natural egoism tends to make me view things from an angle that is definitely favorable to myself. Imagination furthers this process and, confused by a lack of landmarks and points of reference, ends by mistaking wishes for reality and launches out into a world of incoherence packed with suffering and absurdity, where logic has no place. Notwithstanding the petty agitation resulting from all this, together with my superficial and evil impulses, I still feel that there are some true sentiments in the depths of my soul, arising from that innate sense of justice which every man possesses in his inmost heart.

I have often tried to understand the point of view of the others, and to explain to myself their anger, but I have not succeeded, because it is impossible for me to look at my own actions as a simple spectator, taking into account only the brutal facts, overwhelming though they may be. Each time I go back over what happened, not only my own actions but all the things that preceded them — my thoughts, intentions, states of mind — I find it absolutely impossible to describe, because the whole is too complex. These events hold me in their grip and create a certain impression in which nothing can be understood clearly. It is very difficult for me to record my thoughts, because although they run deep, I don't know how to express them. Furthermore, I am haunted by the fear of meeting with an ironic smile or a sarcastic reaction. Is this literature? Regardless of what anyone may think, and because I am writing these lines not for a relentless judge but for compassionate friends who are well disposed toward me, I shall say frankly all that I experienced during those moments that determined my fate. If what I write turns out to be nothing more than a jumble of meaningless words, the product of an unhinged imagination, I shall at least have the merit of honesty.

People have often said to me, "You had everything to make you happy. It is hard to understand how a boy like you, coming from such a fine family, could end up like this." Such an introduction is followed by a series of more or less unflattering reflections, sprinkled with recurring expressions such as "lazy... insatiable... always wanting more." *How untrue these explanations are!* As if the resolve to commit a crime did not have much deeper roots!

Do you wonder how I ended up like this? To be honest, I feel that I have never been free, really free to choose one way or the other. Naturally weak, I was wayward, lethargic, easily led, and had many needs. These factors combined to create a lifestyle which, though not luxurious, cushioned me from contact with the harder realities which are the lot of many. But the deepest cause, I think, for my attitude toward life, was the education I received. I do not think it indiscreet to speak here of what is presently being proclaimed from the rooftops, namely, that *my parents did not get along with one another.* This made our family life utterly wretched. Violent screaming and shouting at times of crisis would be followed by periods of acute embarrassment and frigid formality. *There was no respect, no love.*

My father, full of charm when with strangers, was in truth sarcastic, proud and cynical. An atheist as far as one can be, he felt a disgust with life, which, in spite of his professional success, had brought him nothing but disappointment and disillusion. From my earliest years I fed on his maxims. Obviously it could hardly have been otherwise. Looking around me for examples, I shaped my conduct on that of the stronger character. And so, to sum up, the result was cynicism, amorality, and scorn for humanity, developing easily in a nature well adapted to his philosophy, and ridden with all the needs created by the milieu in which I lived.

I knew for a long time that I would end up badly. I saw very clearly that on the day when I should be free to follow my own way, I would be incapable of acting uprightly. I was a disturbed, unbalanced, and deeply unhappy person. I married because, in the first place, my wife was pregnant, and then too because I had found a semblance of warmth in my new family... I did not love my wife, but we got along well and peaceably. My child I did love. But what is a child when one is twenty and has no moral stability?

I separated from my wife because my mother asked me to, ostensibly because of racial questions but primarily because she realized that we were not suited to each other; in this she was perfectly correct. I have to admit that with or without my mother's intervention we would have ended in divorce.

I found myself alone once more in Saint-Germain-en-Laye (in my mother's home), more unbalanced than ever as a result of this experience which left me with considerable remorse. My father had shrugged off all further family responsibilities and had skulked into a remote corner by himself. My mother, brave and devoted, but marked by years of a married life which was such in name only, was somewhat lacking in warmth and a capacity for intimacy. As we had been before, so we were now — like two strangers. We loved each other, but were embarrassed at being together. She wanted to help me and did so, if not in a reasonable way, at least with her mother's love which, without being outwardly expressed, was nonetheless strong and true. I tried to work — for one month. At the first failure, I gave up completely, and this was the beginning of the sequence of events precipitated by what I might call a sense of fatality past redeeming. Far from being blind, I knew very well where it was leading me. "The fathers have eaten sour grapes, the teeth of the children are on edge." I might have heard at that moment, "Take up your cross, Jacques, by accepting your responsibilities and your duties." But how could I hear a voice which only murmured from the hidden spring, when I was deafened with the roar of an ill-regulated life?

*Free? No, I was not.* Everything conspired to make me flee, to take the broad road leading to perdition. With each passing day the net tightened around me, the net which was to stifle me in the end. A hunted soul! My wife was a living reproach to me because I had abandoned her. My mother, seeing the sorry success of my work, had driven me from her home. Then there were the business associates to whom I had to render accounts — and what accounts — since I had squandered my money on a car! What was I to do? "Oh, it's very simple," they told me. "Sell the car, pay your debts, return to your wife, swallow your pride and go out and look for a job." But where would I get the strength to make such a costly decision? Would I get it from the cynicism, the nihilism that had been inculcated in me? And what would be the point of such a sacrifice, since I was convinced that ultimate chaos was sure to defeat all my schemes, that nothing in this world is in the end either good or evil, that only feelings have value? No, flight was preferable, and what could be more romantic, adventurous and seductive than the suggestion of the friend who whispered in my ear the siren call to a free life, alone in my little boat on the high seas?

This thought was like a limpid stream trickling over the dry sand of my desert. I drank of it, and my thirst was quenched. I would be far from men, whom I did not love. What a marvelous way to escape boredom!

It only remained to put the plan into action. At first a person dreams; nothing appears distinctly. Then, the reality strikes you. You have to deal with it, and take steps. A boat is expensive. I could see at once that I would have to plan how to obtain one. There was only one way — to steal.

"Stop!" you will say to me. "Up to now, it was only a dream, foolish but still acceptable. But to pass from the life of an honest man to that of a criminal so suddenly, without remorse, without any qualms of conscience! You must have had some reaction, some drawing back!"

No, I accepted the idea of stealing without any reflex at all, or scarcely any. This was the natural consequence of my way of seeing things. It was not on that day that I became a criminal; it was long before. I was only putting into practice *what lay latent within me*, when the occasion presented itself. I would have done nothing that led to ultimate delinquency had I discovered an ideal. It wasn't that stealing attracted me. All I needed was a goal beyond purely vegetal ambitions. A mere nothing could have saved me...

"But," you will say, "since you so easily accepted the idea of stealing, why not the same for murder?"

Ah, yes! To be consistent, I ought to have accepted any kind of crime, at least "in principle." A hundred and fifty pounds of humanity are worth no more than a hundred and fifty pounds of beef. But no, I had this weakness in my philosophical system. A murder works on one's imagination. Much evil follows on this, and whether one likes it or not one maintains a certain amount of sensitivity, a weakness transmitted through education and the development of culture.

This idea of aggression once envisaged, even though it left my conscience unaffected, did disturb me as far as social consequences were concerned. There is a psychosis of fear. As a bird fascinated by a snake can no longer move, as the mountain climber seized with an attack of vertigo hurls himself down of his own accord, *one ends by being horribly obsessed by an idea*, to the point where all ability to reflect is lost and one can only be delivered from the evil by surrendering to it.

Then came the pacing back and forth in front of the money-changer's shop. I went there filled with courage, left, returned again after ten minutes, then went away again. There was the abandonment of my two friends, who were supposed to be there precisely to give me courage by their presence. I couldn't eat or sleep. When the crucial moment arrived, no force would have been powerful enough to dispel this criminal obsession. Then, the tragedy began. I entered the shop like a madman, eyes haggard, an evil air about me. I had to be liberated. Everything that had been planned in advance vanished from my mind; I moved like an automaton. I attacked the money-changer to no purpose. Even with partial success I would have gained nothing, since the money wasn't there. I struck the man, and picked up a few bills lying nearby.

Panic stricken, I fired a single bullet and wounded my finger. I felt nothing for the moment, anesthetized by fear.

I left the shop. A passerby saw me and cried out. I ran past my car, never thinking of getting in. I fled, they tracked me down, struck me, shouted. A single refrain pounded through what was left of my brain: *"What have I done? What have I done?"* And then followed an exchange of gunshots, the murder, and the arrest of a savage beast who was acting with the reflexes which had been bequeathed to him by his forebears and which sprang up in the moment of peril. After that... oh well!... prison.

> Later, in a letter to his mother-in-law, Madame Polack, he
> returned to his actions and their motivation. He judged the
> law.

Too often law and morality are confused. If I have done something evil, I know it. But the chief thing I know is *how* I have acted. I know very well that I was not "free" and that if I were free, I would not have done what I did even if, sooner or later, I had fallen to the bottom of the social scale. This is not where my true culpability lies. The actions which have brought me here are not the most grievous elements in this affair.

> Clearly, it is not a question of the objective facts, which are atrocious and irreparable, but of Fesch's profound responsibility. He feels that this is on another level.

The things I reproach myself for are of another order, and if one day I am judged in truth, it will be for them that I shall be weighed in the balance. Pierrette, Veronica... For these I shall have to answer.

How is it that a prisoner condemned to the ultimate penalty should not be able to accept it? Quite simply because it is a man who does not exist who has been judged, a man who is assumed to have been free, balanced and acting in full consciousness; while the prisoner knows very well that he was none of these things. Albeit he is unable to explain his actions clearly even to himself, his sense of justice is wounded... His actions deserve condemnation, but perhaps he himself deserves it less. What has happened to him may be a matter of interest, but one should not be led astray by it. There is nothing to prove that the evil which was in him will not surface again. This viewpoint would be fairer, and closer to the truth.

# CHAPTER 5

# CONVERSION

Jacques Fesch had received a traditional Christian education. It did indeed leave its mark on him, but very early, under the influence of his father, the effects wore off.

We mentioned that soon after his arrival in prison the chaplain came to visit him. Jacques sent him away courteously, declaring that he "had no faith."

However, a slow maturing process had begun. Confronted with himself in silence and complete solitude, Fesch was to rediscover that self in rediscovering his God. It was his hour. The assassin did not turn away from it.

Some believers may think that this reaction was the obvious one. When you are stripped of everything, how can you help turning to God? But no, it was not obvious. It is no easier to allow yourself to be led by the hand and drawn out of darkness when you are in prison, than when you are free.

The interior liberation, the new birth which was about to take place, was an event of prime importance in the life of Fesch. This egoist-turned-criminal was willing, for the first time in his life, to forget himself, to love, to give himself. At this moment, when Fesch's world lay in ruins, God appealed to him, and the merit of this unfortunate man without merit was that he was willing to listen to the voice he heard at the heart of his distress. That voice was to lead him — for he would never cease to listen to it — in ever increasing joy, up to the day of his atrocious death.

Fesch was helped — always with respect for his freedom — by

the chaplain, who visited him and loaned him books. He was helped by the friendship, letters, and prayers of a former childhood friend of Pierrette's, now a religious named Brother Thomas. He was helped above all by his lawyer, Paul Baudet, a sincere Christian who devoted himself personally to those whom he served. Catholics believe in what they call the mystery of "the communion of saints," that is, they believe that all Christians, all men of good will, are members of one immense body, who is Christ. They know that the life circulating in this body, which is the life of God Himself, is shared by all the members, from the strongest to the weakest.

I have to insist on this further point: we should not think Jacques Fesch was converted in a day. Reading the letters which follow might give us that impression, so tremendous is the distance between these letters and the account of the murder immediately preceding them. Neither is it necessary to believe, as we mentioned above, that this outcome was inevitable, with Jacques, deprived of his liberty and of all human hope, turning naturally to the one possible way out, God. There are, unfortunately, many assassins, many prisoners, who spend decades in jail, yet how many of them are "converted"? The fact is, Jacques' journey toward the Light extended over a full year. This is a long, very long time for someone who, alone and inactive, has only one thing to do: to reflect. On the other hand, at the beginning of his detention Fesch was quite sure he would not get the death sentence and that one day, since he was young, he would regain his freedom.

As we read the letters in sequence, it is easy to define the stages of his conversion. Shortly after the tragedy, Jacques Fesch, in the solitude of his cell, undertook to rediscover his Christian faith and to return to it (see the letters of March 18 and 24 and August 24, 1954, in *Cell 18*). In October, 1954, an interior transformation took place after he had read a book on the Blessed Virgin Mary (this is described in the unpublished letters to his wife).

This was only the beginning of his conversion, but this is where Baudet places it, that is, at the end of the eighth month of his detention, in October, 1954. This stage is clearly described by Jacques in a passage of his letter of June 8, 1955:

Little by little I was led to change my ideas. I was no longer certain that God did not exist. I began to be open to Him, though I did not as yet have faith. I tried to believe with my reason, without praying, or praying ever so little!

This stage was completed on the memorable night of his conversion, at the beginning of March, 1955. Let us listen to Jacques once more, as he continues the same passage quoted above:

And then, at the end of my first year in prison, a powerful wave of emotion swept over me, causing deep and brutal suffering. Within the space of a few hours, I came into possession of faith, with absolute certainty. I believed, and could no longer understand how I had ever not believed. Grace had come to me. A great joy flooded my soul, and above all a deep peace. In a few instants everything had become clear. It was a very strong, sensible joy that I felt. I tend now to try, perhaps excessively, to recapture it; actually, the essential thing is not emotion, but faith.

On this same night of his conversion, Jacques Fesch heard an interior voice urging him to be converted. Later, he heard this compelling voice a second time (see Jacques' words to his lawyer, Baudet, in Chapter 11 of *Light Over the Scaffold*).

If I have quoted these passages, which you will encounter later in their context, it is because they are essential. They show that we are dealing with an authentic conversion. Previously, efforts to believe had been fruitless. Faith is not a kind of autosuggestion. It is a grace coming from God, the grace of a mysterious encounter with Someone. It is beyond reasoning and emotion (which certainly is not to say that these cannot be present); it is the birth of a new man. Jacques Fesch would never be the same again. This is how he put it in his very first letter to his religious friend Brother Thomas:

*2. Light Over the Scaffold*

*Tuesday, April 26, 1955*

My brother, "Ask and it will be given you, seek and you will find, knock, and it will be opened to you" (Mt 7:7). I am ashamed not to have answered your long letter of last year, but at that time I did not understand what you were saying. Now, I BELIEVE, and I have confidence in God. I thank you from the bottom of my heart for your many prayers, and may this little note bring you a bit of joy. I'll write again later.

Your brother in God,
Jacques

CHAPTER 6

# A NEW LIFE

At the end of his first year in prison, Jacques Fesch opened himself to the life of faith. Since his response was a total one, he entered quickly into an authentic experience of God, an experience which is personal for each of us, and always unique. Only one who has lived through it can describe it.

*Saturday, May 14, 1955*

My brother Thomas [his religious friend],

Thank you for your long letter. It did me so much good, and united me to you so closely. How I wish I could tell you all that I feel in the depths of my being! But I've never been much good at expressing myself.

That stone of pride and egoism which has served me as a heart is sterile, so sterile. I am begging the Lord to give me a heart of flesh, and from the depths of the abyss I cry out to Him to hear my voice. With all my strength I thank Him for having had pity on my distress and for responding to my crimes with His love.

How well you understand me! Yes, an immense grief and an immense joy sweep over the soul together, and for the first time I have wept tears of joy, knowing with certitude that God has forgiven me and that now Christ lives in me through my suffering and my love… You see, I am opening my soul to you. I admit that I am still a very tepid Christian, repentant certainly, and full of good will, but without much will power. I so need His love, strength, and compassion.

As you wrote me last year, "the dried blood still burns in my face." I often fall back into a kind of apathy and resignation, and I am unhappy because I sense at these times that all joy has gone and that there is nothing left but despair. I beg Him to live in me always, to help and enlighten me, and to give me the strength to accept the sufferings His mercy has willed to send me for the sake of my birth into the light, to me, who helped to sink the nails into His hands. But with Him there is mercy, and because of His law I have hoped in Him.

Brother, I need your prayers. I pray for you, but my prayer is a very feeble light that scarcely pierces the shadows. Even so, may it be pleasing to God.

For the time being, I can write to you as often as I want; we are allowed sixty lines a day. And I can receive as many letters as are sent to me. Once a person is condemned, though, the limit is one letter a month and that only from the family. I shall be judged in a few months now, perhaps even in June. Then, little brother, we will have to be content with being united in prayer.

I receive Holy Communion once a month. I do not have permission to assist at Mass, being under maximum security, but for those in my situation the chaplain is obliged to celebrate a special Mass individually for each one.

In comparison with your life as you described it to me in your last letter, the rules here are less strict, except for the perpetual solitude and being confined within four walls. It's hard to get used to it. Without God, the cell would be such a pit of darkness and despair that a person could easily rot away or else turn into a wild beast.

I have a fine lawyer, to whom I owe a great deal. He has encouraged me steadily throughout this year of gloom, and directed me toward the path of light…

As for Pierrette, she has gone through some very hard moments and still is…

I embrace you in Christ Jesus.

Your brother,
Jacques

In his letters, especially those to his monk friend, Jacques
often quotes Sacred Scripture and spiritual authors. This
is because he has been reading and meditating a great deal.
He has thus become familiar with these texts, which form
his daily nourishment.

*Wednesday, June 8, 1955*

My dear Brother,

"Taste with your heart's palate the food of life." I have just
received Communion; it is a great joy! "It is no longer I who live, but
Christ lives in me." And just think, this morning, at eight o'clock,
when you were making your thanksgiving, I united myself to you
through prayer and Communion. [In one of his letters Brother Thomas had told him the times of his various spiritual exercises. Jacques
would very often unite himself in thought and prayer to this very dear
friend.]

From now on, I shall be able to receive Communion twice a
month instead of once only, and perhaps oftener if the chaplain is able
to do it. For the first time, I really have the feeling that I am beginning
to live. I have peace, and my life has meaning, whereas before I was
dead while still alive. "I do not wish the death of the sinner, but that he
should turn from his evil ways and live." But what struggles to reach
that point! What consequences I'm going to have to suffer for the rest
of my life: the death of a man, the unhappiness of a woman and a
young girl, two children grieving, an orphan! How much evil I have
spread around me through my egoism and recklessness. "Ah, Lord,
behold the guilty ones who stand before you confessing their crimes!"
(St. Augustine).

Yes, it is He who loved me first, when I had done nothing to
deserve His love. He has filled me with graces and given me a brother
to love. Do you know, every day I read your letters over, and draw so
much strength from them! The thought of you never leaves me, and I

am convinced that a few years from now we shall meet face to face:
"You have seen your brother, you have seen your God." In your last
letter you spoke of coming to bring me Communion, wherever I might
be. Do you really think it would be possible? How happy I should be!

Little brother, you asked me to tell you when and how I discovered the God of love. First I must tell you what I was like before, so
that you will understand better. During the six or seven years when I
lived without faith, I did evil, much evil, less through deliberate malice than through heedlessness, egoism and hardness of heart. I was
incapable of loving anyone. Father, mother, wife, child — I was indifferent to them all. I felt no warmth of emotion for anyone or anything,
unless perhaps it was music. My activities consisted in the mere mechanical proliferation of egotistical sensations, and this to an absolute
degree. I did exactly as I pleased, without the slightest concern for
others. In me, there was no life — "He who does not love abides in
death" (Jn 3:13-18) — but great anguish.

My conviction that God did not exist grew stronger and more
deeply entrenched in my soul. I ignored Him completely. When anyone spoke to me of Him, I would retort, "A fine figment of the imagination... a palliative for those who suffer... the religion of slaves, of
the underdog." I did nothing with spontaneity or enthusiasm — I was
a real robot. And yet I was unhappy. I knew it, and I tried to find my
happiness in being miserable.

What happened was only the logical consequence of all the evil
seething within me. I assaulted the money-changer in order to free
myself. It was as if I were absolutely sure of the end result. You see,
I have the impression now that I was bound to do what I did, that I was
the plaything of higher forces. I understood nothing any more. I had
reached the point where one easily commits suicide. "If anyone walks
in the daylight he does not stumble, because he has the light, but if he
walks by night he falls, because there is no light in him" (St. John).

According to the witnesses, during the tragedy my face was like
that of a raging tiger. In one second, all the evil within me surfaced.
As for me, I can remember nothing. I saw nothing, I acted like one
possessed. And after all this came despair. I didn't understand your
first letter, I didn't believe!

After some months in prison, urged on tirelessly by my lawyer, I tried to believe. Little by little, I was led to change my ideas. I was no longer certain that God did not exist. I began to be open to Him, though I did not as yet have faith. I tried to believe with my reason, without praying, or praying ever so little!

Then, at the end of my first year in prison, a powerful wave of emotion swept over me, causing deep and brutal suffering. Within the space of a few hours I came into possession of faith, with absolute certitude. I believed, and could no longer understand how I had ever not believed. Grace had come to me. A great joy flooded my soul, and above all, a deep peace. In a few instants, everything had become clear. It was a very strong, sensible joy that I felt. I tend now, perhaps excessively, to try to recapture it; actually, the essential thing is not emotion, but faith. "But this belongs to night." Everything is lightsome now, but I still have so far to go!

Little brother, I can't go beyond sixty lines, and must leave you. I unite myself with you each morning at the hours you mentioned...

I embrace you in Christ Jesus.

> Your brother in God,
> Jacques

Fesch's wife Pierrette had no faith. Jacques, having rediscovered the God he had rejected, longed for only one thing: that she in her turn might be given this light, and through it win peace. He could not remain silent. At the risk of aggravating his wife, he returned to the subject "in season and out of season."

Faith is not a means but an end, and your formal refusal of it comes only from a lack of humility. You are refusing the most powerful help that can be given! All the same, I understand this very well, because I used to have the same reactions. We do not want to see. We need to take only a little step, but it means leaving behind our bitterness and pride and surrendering to the will of the One who can do everything. You especially, Minouche, who are so unhappy and so alone!

"Come to me, all you who labor and are burdened, and I will give you rest..." What more do we want? What are we all chasing after, if not relief from our misery? Oh Creator, have pity on your creatures. Consider that we do not understand ourselves, that we do not know what we want, that we have no idea what we are asking for. Lord, give us light. How hard it is to love someone who does not love you, to open to someone who does not knock, to give health to someone who enjoys being sick and cultivates illness! "Have pity on those who have no pity for themselves!" Forgive me, Treasure, for boring you with all these long sentences which will tire you out all over again...

*Monday, August 22, 1955*

Dear little brother,

I think it's very unfair of me to complain, when I have so much to be forgiven for myself. Yes! I ought to accept this purifying trial gladly, and thank the Lord for having enlightened me and brought me back to the sheepfold. What does the loss of liberty matter, and passing sufferings, if we are admitted among the elect! Only, human nature is weak; I am blind; memories of the past keep sweeping over me like blasts of hot air until I can think of nothing but what I have lost.

But you know, these periodic attacks of depression are becoming rarer and rarer, less and less intense. What used to be my reason for living leaves a bitter taste in my mouth. Now I feel a new inner strength, an absolute certainty that my only salvation and duty lie in giving myself wholly to His love. But I don't succeed in doing this very well. It's hard to wriggle out of the net of one's vices...

You see, when I did not believe, I imagined that faith was merely autosuggestion, and that a person could come to belief simply by saying "I believe." My reasoning was based on my feeling that understanding was impossible, and on the contradictions I thought I had observed. I was sure that this reasoning was logical and true, and so it strengthened my conviction that God did not exist.

Now, I no longer understand how I ever managed not to believe. It all seems so far away. The most judicious reasonings and deductions, which used to attract me, now seem vain and above all "highly improbable"!

Because of this, I can see that faith is truly a gift of God. One believes with the heart, without knowing why or even seeking to know. The intimate certitude that fills one is enough. Of all things, love is the most powerful...

I am aware of my obligations, at least to my little girl: to take on her spiritual education if I am able, and to repair the evil I have done, even by the sacrifice of my own person...

Little brother, I remain always united to you through prayer and Holy Communion, which I am now receiving once a week, and in thought I never leave you.

I'll write again soon; I embrace you in Christ Jesus.

Your brother,

Jacques

*Tuesday, November 15, 1955*

Dear little brother,

It's a long time since I have written. Excuses? I have none. I left for Orleans some time ago and returned immediately, since for a number of reasons the prosecutor did not want to keep me down there. So I shall remain here for about one more year, if not longer.

Forgive me for not having written you. I'm afraid you must have been worried. To tell the truth, and I admit it to my deep shame, for some time things have not been going well, first of all physically, due to weakness and anemia which have made me fairly miserable, particularly in this perpetual isolation. Then, morally, an upset which is actually over now but which left me disoriented for some time.[1]

Instead of referring everything to God so as to be strengthened by faith, I made the great mistake of examining my situation from a human angle, looking to the future, and wishing vehemently for a kinder fate from a worldly point of view. Of course easy solutions came to mind, acceptable at first so to speak, and then ones that were more and more evil, drawing me once more into the quagmire of sin. In the end, little brother, I swept all these villainous thoughts aside and climbed back up the slope with determination. When my will no longer tended toward God, my imagination was violently assailed, and my fall was imminent.

This morning I received Communion and talked with the chaplain for a long time. Each time he speaks with me I feel stronger. He is so patient and gentle and has such an understanding of human weaknesses!

Very dear little brother, I will write you a little more very soon. I embrace you in Christ Jesus.

                                                              Jacques

---

[1] A reference to the dark night in which Jacques was plunged "for about six months" after his conversion. Jacques, too recently converted, did not understand this new state common to all mystics. (See *In Five Hours I Shall See Jesus*, Jacques' Journal, August 3, 1957 [Le Sarment, Fayard, 1989].)

CHAPTER 7

# GROWTH

Jacques' faith was being purified inexorably by God, because the time was short. Following upon this testing came joy, a joy Jacques was almost afraid to welcome. But God knows what is best for His own, what most fitting for the very personal character of each one. Thanks to Jacques' state of "enclosure" — stricter than that of a Carthusian — God nourished him with authentic contemplation.

In the evenings, when the silence of the night increased his solitude, Jacques knew still more intimately both the experience of love and the plunge into his conscious misery, his shadow side. These are the purifying stages of the divine action upon the soul beloved of God, whose beauty He desires at all cost. As a log licked by the flames must be purged of all dross before becoming incandescent, must be stripped of its very self to be enriched by the fire, the soul is now at the center of the hearth, and the hearth knows what it will do to it. Jacques let himself be transformed, kindled "within" by the Spirit, enlightened "without" by the Sacred Scriptures which nourished him day by day.

Jacques knew peace, but this peace also rekindled a human hope. Now this "human" hope of liberation had also to be relinquished, sooner or later, given up along

with all the rest. Gently, without haste, God would re-
move all fear about the past, which was no more, all fear
of men's judgment, and also any too human sense of security. At the same time, the tangible experience of his misery continued to return, to the point of nausea.

Everything had to be created anew, in its entirety.
And everything would be recreated. Jacques knew this.
He dreaded it, he longed for it, and he willed it. He loved,
and allowed himself to be loved.

*Monday, December 5, 1955*

Dear little brother,
"Now is the hour for us to wake from sleep; our salvation is near
at hand" (Paul [Rm] 13:11, 14).
What a long, dark night I have just passed through![1] But now for
some time things have been going better, much better. I have driven
the shadows away and once more found joy in the love of Christ.

Thank you for your long letter. Yes, little brother, you are always faithful, kind, and persevering, and I don't know what you must
think of this abominable tepidity of mine for some time past. "Let the
sluggish soul awake at last..." But don't worry about me any more,
and forgive my inexcusable silence.

Thank you with all my heart for the wise advice you gave me
about Pierrette. It is obviously my duty to help her with understanding
and charity. You see, I told her that she was absolutely free to choose
the way she judged best for herself and her little girl. She knows that
I am her support now, only a moral support at the moment, but one she
can cling to night and day. She loves with all the ardor of her passion,
and it is a great proof of love to go on hoping as firmly as she does, in
the total night which hangs over our horizon at present! It's the miracle
of love that is stronger than separation or death, and that still goes on
hoping when there is nothing in view but despair.

---

[1] Jacques is alluding to the spiritual night mentioned in the preceding letter.

Of course now and then I sense that she hesitates and weakens as her family cares and her perpetual insecurity bear down upon her. But I shall always let her make her own decisions. She will act according to her strength and her power of resistance. I don't feel I have the right to refuse her anything, or to oblige her to anything. She is beginning to search for God, but it's hard… It is necessary for her to believe, especially in the face of such demands on her strength and courage! Only with faith will she be able to make a valid choice, one way or the other…

You ask me for details about prison life. It is very simple, little brother. We are always in our cells except for a half-hour's walk each day, which is taken in solitude. One half hour in the parlor a week, one package a month, and that's it. We get up at seven and lights are out at seven. My occupations are limited to reading: three books a week, or more if they come my way, and mail. It was very hard in the beginning, but gradually I'm getting used to it.

Obviously, my health reacts to such a routine, with general weakness and anemia. My heart contracts, and from time to time I have a bit of pain. The most irksome thing for me is the lack of living space. But then, I can't complain. People help me, and I don't suffer from hunger. I have no Bible at the moment, but I'm hoping to receive one soon…

Little by little the prisoner organized his prayer life and chose religious exercises which he carried out during the daylight hours, often arranging his schedule to match that of his friend, who was "enclosed" for the glory of God.

Each morning I read my Mass at the hour when you told me that you assist at it, and once a week, on Tuesday or Wednesday, the chaplain celebrates Mass in a separate cell. I attend it all alone, since I am under maximum security. During the day I read or write. The chaplain often lends me books. I have just finished a life of St. Teresa of Avila, which I found illuminating.

And then, little brother, I try very awkwardly to talk with God as often as possible, thinking about what I have read, or praying to Him.

Right now, I am making the Way of the Cross in spirit, trying to fix my attention as well as I can on the scenes, and doing my best to understand them. I admit that until now I never understood the Passion. As I reflect, new aspects strike me. I believe it's a good devotion. When evening comes, at seven o'clock, plunged in darkness, I end my day by reciting "Sunday Compline," which you too must surely be reciting at that time.

You see, I'm feeling my way, trying to live as far as possible in union with Christ, but I am so weak and spineless! My attempts at adoration often resemble the motions of a mechanical toy when it is about to run down. If you give it a push, it jerks once or twice more, then stops...

Yet at present I feel much stronger, even joyous. I am conscious of all the riches God places within us, if we ask Him. I marvel at the greatness of His mercy and the infinite love He has for us. I believe, and entrust my sufferings and sorrows to Christ's understanding. "How sweet His yoke is!" And then, in the silence of my cell, I look at the cross, and I'm not alone any more. "The Lord was not in the wind... He was not in the earthquake... He was not in the roaring of the sea... but He was in the gentle murmur of the brook and He spoke to Elijah. . ." Let us listen to this still, small voice: "I have loved you with an everlasting love and I have drawn you in My mercy."

Till next time, little brother. I'll write you again for your feast. I embrace you in Christ Jesus.

Your brother in God,
Jacques

Our picture of Jacques would be incomplete if we had only the witness of his letters to his religious friend, where the topic is almost exclusively his interior transformation. In spite of this extraordinary spiritual experience, he remained in fact very "human." When first imprisoned, he wrote to his mother-in-law, Madame Polack,[2] with whom he corresponded almost daily after his condemnation:

I often think, you know, of my little girl. I should love to have her near me. Perhaps I need this trial to open my eyes! [...] How I should love to have gone on the camping trip with my little girl. I think of her very, very often, and I am forever wondering what devastating effect my story will have on her soul. No father to help and protect her, but instead, a father who will doubtless be criticized in her presence, and who is certainly responsible for leaving her a fearful legacy, one which will expose her to the suspicion of others.

At Christmas Jacques was seriously startled by his lawyer, who, fearing that his "delight" in God might block his spiritual progress, questioned him about the joy which he experienced inwardly, or was seeking.

*December 21, 1955: Feast of St. Thomas*

Dear little brother,

As I promised, I am writing for your feast and also for Christmas. In four days, a Savior will be given to us.

Here, alas, Christmas is just another day. There is no question of Midnight Mass, not even of Mass on the day itself. At seven o'clock we are in total darkness, so much so that I cannot even read the Office. This morning I went to Mass, and I asked your patron saint to bring you joy and perseverance all year through.

Little brother, is joy indispensable, or not? Should we consider

---

[2] It is to Madame Polack that we owe the return of Jacques Fesch's body (an exceptional measure at the time), for burial in the family vault in the cemetery in Saint-Germain-en-Laye.

it as a grace that is strengthening but somewhat non-essential? For my part, you see, when joy fails me, I feel totally helpless, and it is then that "the old man" rises up with incredible strength! All that I thought was far behind me once more confronts me, with the same virulence as before and without even the slightest attenuation as far as its seriousness goes. I have to struggle with all my might in order to repulse these evil desires. Yet here I am locked up, without any concrete temptations. What would I be if I were outside? I believe, to my utter shame, that I would fall back into the same mistakes, at least momentarily. "The dog returns to its vomit." How weak the flesh is! At these moments of depression I pray more than usual perhaps, but so badly. I always feel that I'm alone, and that all my efforts are in vain. So much so, that in the end my whole prayer is nothing but a plea for strength and joy.

According to my lawyer, all this is a bit irrelevant, and he thinks my religion consists in looking for sweetness to compensate for the suffering I have to endure. Perhaps he is right? Yet I read in the life of St. Francis of Assisi that this great saint made joy one of the basic elements of his rule: "Poverty, chastity, and joy." And to those who were amazed to see him perpetually dancing for joy, he replied that joy springs from a pure heart and constancy in prayer. Little brother, is joy good or bad? Should we seek it, or simply accept it when it comes with infinite thanks, as a grace we don't deserve? Yet here in this place things would be pretty grim without joy. Whether I like it or not, without my realizing it, I sometimes feel an overwhelming wave of hatred sweep over me, for everything that plagues and torments me. And if I were to entertain this, or simply let it take over, I believe the consequences could be horrendous. This is the road to becoming a brute, a killer... "Oh Lord, I fear everything from my natural perversity, but I hope for everything from Your goodness!" I read in the Letters of St. Peter that it is good to suffer unjustly, but what merit is there in suffering when we deserve it? Even the pagans do this. And to think that I am not even capable yet of accepting in my heart the punishment I have so richly deserved. Pride and sloth!

A few days ago the chaplain brought me the Bible. I have only read part, since he couldn't lend it to me for very long. I read the first books as far as Ezra, the Epistles and the Apocalypse. At first I was a bit scandalized by the customs of former days. God's laws struck me as quite harsh, not like those of Christ. As I thought about it, I decided that God had given His laws with a view to the state of development of the men of those times. But apart from a few biblical figures like Joseph and Job, the rest seemed so materialistic to me that I was shocked. I would rather read the Gospels and Epistles, and the lives of the saints. I can draw more strength from these. I think the chaplain is going to lend me the life of St. Dominic this week.

Concerning the trial, little brother, there is nothing new. The investigation is taking its course. It is perhaps going better than the last time [actually this was the second investigation on the same evidence, the first having been annulled by the Supreme Court of Appeal because of a legal irregularity]. From a more human point of view, the judge delayed much longer over the "why" of the affair, and I think that, all things considered, I shall be judged with the highest degree of indulgence. If all goes well, I'll get twenty years. Otherwise, life. Either way, it doesn't make much difference. These days, people are released more easily than they deserve. The best sentence I could get, on condition of good conduct, would be ten years. Ten years of hard labor, four of them spent in solitary confinement! The law is hard.

But still, little brother, if I am willing, I can profit considerably from these ten years. Anyhow, to be a walking corpse, which is what I was when I was free, is worse than to be alive and locked up. "'For three years I have come looking for fruit from this fig tree, and have found none. Cut it down!' — 'Lord, leave it for this one year more, that I may dig around it and dung it. Perhaps then you will find some fruit. If not, cut it down.'"

Dear little brother, Merry Christmas! I'll write you again in January.

I embrace you in Christ Jesus.

Jacques

Yes, the Christian ought to cultivate joy. Jacques Fesch's reflections on this joy touch the very heart of the Good News brought by Christ. The difference between other religions and the Christian religion is precisely joy, springing, for man, from the heart of Christ on the cross. This is what makes the Gospel "good news." Under the ancient Jewish law "the just" were saved by their total observance of the law. At best this form of morality imprisoned man the sinner within man the pardoned, but he was always the same man... And God, they thought, would judge those who had broken the law, on the last day if not before.

"Master, who has sinned, this man or his parents, that he should be born blind?" the apostles asked Jesus. Under the new law of love, men are saved only by the blood of Christ, and neither their sin nor the sin of their parents renders them accursed of God. Just or sinners, all are justified by the blood of Christ and not by the works of the law. But one must accept this blood and allow oneself to be regenerated by it. That is enough. On each man's last day, it is not God who will judge his sins, but the man himself. He will declare that he is guilty of this blood, if it has been shed in vain for him through his refusal to accept it. This is the true sin of man: his refusal.

Nietzsche was right: "I will believe in their Savior when men act as if they have been saved!" Two thousand years of Christianity should not make us proud of our conquests. We have to admit that the world in which suffering and death hold sway, a world where men search in the dark for the One who will bring them a light so that their night may be endurable, or deliver them from themselves — this world needs to "see" Christians who believe with their whole being that Christ has done everything, redeemed all, accomplished all, and that the "justice" of man has definitively been achieved for all who are willing to accept it. The sole witness to be given is not that of heroic virtue, which is often impossible, but that of joy in the fact that Christ has done all, He alone.

In the Christian religion there is neither Jew nor Greek, free man nor slave, just nor sinners. There are no more verities "to be believed" or morality "to practice" in order to be saved... There is only a man's heart to be opened to this God who has come to bring salvation and joy. "Love, and do what you will," St. Augustine of Hippo advised. There remains only the immense assembly of those who have been justified in the Blood of the Lamb.

Fesch would live all this in its fullness a few weeks before his death and would be filled with joy. But he had yet to learn Christ in His spirit, His flesh and His blood, and he continued to struggle...

*Tuesday, January 31, 1956*

Dear little brother,

Here we are at the last day of the month and I haven't yet written you. Don't think I've forgotten you, I am faithful to our rendezvous, but for some time lately my mind has been a bit numb, probably the effect of the grippe and a cold which has been dragging on, and I've put off all correspondence.

Spiritually, things are going very well, and I must admit that your example and your zeal have helped me a lot. Each time weariness attacks me and I rebel against pain, I think of you, living under very difficult conditions accepted voluntarily. Your life is much more difficult than mine, because I am only suffering what I deserve. Didn't St. Peter say, "Let no one suffer as a thief, or a murderer, or a meddler in other peoples' affairs..."?

Actually, I find it very hard to accept my present lot, probably because I'm proud or lazy. It's difficult to be detached from vanities and the bonds of the flesh and the world. "I delight in the law of God, in my inmost self, but I see in my members another law at war with the law of my mind and making me captive to the law of sin which dwells in my members. Wretched man that I am! Who will deliver me from this body of death?" [Rm 7:22-24]. The word of the Lord stands forever. I am trying with all my strength to live as a free man in Jesus Christ, giving Him homage and glory for the infinite gifts He has already bestowed on me. I gain much strength from prayer, from intimate conversation with God, and sometimes I taste how sweet the Lord is! This is a great joy and consolation.

I believe the chaplain has written you, not giving you much hope in regard to the Mass you wanted to celebrate here. The regulations are very strict, especially for those under maximum security.

I heard from Pierrette, who is now living with Denise J. Her parents threw her out again. She managed to find work in an American company and I think she is getting herself organized. Only, how will it all turn out? I worry about this. Her life at present is a dangerous one for a woman alone.

My little girl is with my mother, and has measles and bronchitis. My mother, who had surgery two years ago for a stomach ulcer, has been having violent pains recently, which worries me exceedingly. And my father, at sixty-two, writes me that his sight is failing him, and that he is "going to go out and eat grass." He worries me too, for he is a complete atheist, and hasn't been to confession for at least forty-five years! He suffers much from his solitude, which is both physical and moral... I beg the Blessed Virgin to hear my prayers, she who is at the source of infinite mercy!

At home, we had about as much religion as you would find in a stable, and since I've been here the members of my family have each begun to examine their consciences. Little by little they are growing united again, and renewed. My mother and one of my sisters have already formed a little nucleus. All that remains is for them to bring back my father and my other sister. This will come about, perhaps, if God wills it.

Little brother, I am confiding my joys and sorrows to you in the Lord, so that "He may comfort us in all our afflictions, so that through the comfort with which God comforts us, we too may comfort others, in whatever afflictions they may suffer."

Dear little brother, very soon I will write you again. I leave you with an embrace in Christ Jesus.

Jacques

Jacques Fesch was certainly no poet or mystic by nature. If grace endowed him with these dimensions, it was with a naturally rational, analytical mind that he dissected the "mechanism" of the faith, as a watchmaker handles a watch. He did it with the precision of a Christian who lives what he believes, a theologian who is being taught from within. God and suffering are excellent teachers. Jacques Fesch bears witness to this. The following letter is worthy of the teaching of a St. Paul. If he had been told this, no one would have been more astounded than Fesch. This letter is important. Read it, reread it, several times.

*Saturday, February 11, 1956*

Dear little brother,

"Give thanks to the Lord, for He is good. Let them declare it, who have been redeemed by the Lord." It will soon be one year since the Lord called me in His mercy. As for the exact date of my conversion, I can't put my finger on it. It happened progressively, as I moved from atheism to a very marked, sincere faith, but when I look back I can no longer discern the landmarks along the way. I had been completely indifferent, but one day I realized that I had new eyes, and a view of reality which I had never anticipated was given to me.

Before that, the true God was an indifferent tradition as far as I was concerned. Now, He is all that matters. He is at the center of the world, He rises above my being. He invades me totally, and my spirit cannot escape from Him. A powerful hand has seized me. Where is it?

What has it done to me? I do not know, for His action is not like the action of men, it is unknowable and effective. It constrains me, and I am free. It transforms my being, yet I do not cease to be what I am.

Then comes the struggle — silent, tragic — between what I was and what I have become. For the new creature who has been planted within me calls for a response which I am free to refuse. I have received the principle; I must go on to the consequences. My viewpoint has changed, but my habits of thought and action have not. God has left them as they were. I have to fight, adapt, reconstruct my inner being, and I cannot be at peace unless I accept to fight.

I am amazed and surprised at the change which grace has effected in me. Claudel once described "the state of a man who has been pulled out of his own skin with one yank to be thrust into a strange body in the middle of an unknown world." This is the only comparison I can find to describe my state of complete disarray. I have found peace, but at the same time war. It is a perpetual struggle in which I do gain ground, yet the further I advance the more I perceive my misery and the infinite distance ahead which I must cover. To stand still would be to fall back.

In this radical experience which is overturning my life and marking it indelibly, I perceive an ongoing need for spiritual renewal. Conversion engenders a new outlook, and I am learning that religion is not a matter of consolation but will always, in some sense, involve conversion. But God is here. In Him I have the strength to see and do whatever I must, so as to be conformed to His image. He unites my prayer to His will. The vocation He gives me arouses a prayer within me, which I address to Him.

Little brother, I shall pray for you most specially on Ember Wednesday and Friday of Lent. I understand that these two days are the dearest to you in the whole year! Spend a good Lent, in peace and joy.

I embrace you in Christ.

                                                        Jacques

*Wednesday, April 11, 1956*

Dear little brother,

I promised to write you at the end of Lent so that you would receive my letter for Easter. Forgive this delay. I have had a bit of nervous illness and am still not doing too well. Being confined in a cell for years causes a kind of anguish which is very painful. The worst part is that I haven't come to the end of this regime of solitary confinement. Two more years to go — woe is me!

This morning I received Communion as on all Wednesdays, and I feel more peaceful. It's nothing but a continual succession of ups and downs. I spent the months of January and February in a state of spiritual euphoria which helped greatly in my search for God, and then, from March on, I fell back into complete darkness. At first I was strong with the joy I had experienced for two months, but now I can hardly drag myself along, with sighs and groans and calls for help. God certainly wants to try me, and evidently He thinks this state of abandonment is the most profitable one for my salvation and my future glory...

I read more and more. I have a Bible, and read a passage every day, but it is odd how the same lines can take on different meanings depending on how they are read, and according to the grace within. What is "a torrent of living water" one day is no more than a stock phrase without much meaning the next. I who was convinced a few months ago that it was impossible to read the Gospel without being converted find today that the glowing truths it contains are only such when read with the eyes of grace. "I thank you, Father, because You have hidden these things from the learned and revealed them to little ones."

I hope that you, for your part, had a good Holy Week. I was united with you in the Paschal vigil while reading the rites of the diaconate. Soon you will be a priest!

My mother is very ill now, and there is a fair likelihood that her cancer has metastasized. She suffers quite a bit but has periods of relief. The doctors do not give their opinion. My father comes to see me every week, as adamantly atheistic as ever. And yet, if he wanted to understand the evils which have struck his family — his son in prison, his wife gravely ill, and his daughter divorced after ten years of marriage and two children... He himself feels abandoned, old and unhappy. But he wouldn't for anything in the world admit the fact that his life has been nothing more than one ghastly mistake after another which has landed us all where we are. May the Lord have pity on him and give him the graces he needs in order to die in the dispositions necessary for his salvation.

Dear little brother, forgive me for this letter. You will certainly find it very despondent, and shedding no rays of the light dwelling within me. There is a little cloud over the sun, but I am sure that in time things will go better. I'll write again soon!

I embrace you in Christ Jesus.

Jacques

Without fully understanding what was happening, Jacques continued to undergo a profound transformation. The moments of exaltation and depression he experienced were not simply the natural effect of his painful incarceration. Far more, it was a question of mystical purifications. To the one who loves God and opens his heart to Him without reserve, God sometimes gives the extraordinary grace of quasi-divine joys. Then He withdraws, lest the Christian risk seeking God for his own pleasure rather than for God's sake. His apparent absence is a grievous trial, but also the occasion for the Christian living through this "night" to purify and intensify his faith. If he is faithful, God reveals Himself once more, and leads the one He loves by stages to unending joy.

*Thursday, May 17, 1956*

Dear little brother,

I received your last letter, and also the "Face of Christ" which you sent me. I have wanted to write you for several days but couldn't seem to do it. To tell the truth, for the last two months I have felt very remote, and in a state of torpor and indifference which has worried me.

Today I received Communion and things are going much better, but I'd really like to get out of this miserable state. One good thing about it is that it shows me that of myself I can't do anything, and that if God doesn't help me abundantly I shall remain totally paralyzed in this stagnation. I can't even manage to pray properly. My mind wanders beyond the walls and bars, and I can't concentrate on anything.

Eight or ten months ago I passed through a similar crisis, even worse, and when I recovered my ardor I found it was greater than before. God probably wants to make me understand that what is given me is not due to any merit of mine, as I was inclined to think, but is only the free gift of His mercy. May He have pity on my solitude, unworthy as I am, and fill me with His grace.

I've recently had a certain satisfaction in regard to my father. He is a convinced atheist, who judges that all "this" is nothing but nonsense and absurdity but who, each time he comes to see me, can't help choosing it as the subject of our half-hour's conversation. And he no longer seems so sure that it is all "nonsense." I believe that interiorly he is deeply touched. Such a series of catastrophes have broken upon him that he feels shattered. I try to tell him what religion is, and that there is order and an obvious meaning in the world, but I have no great talent as an orator, and my apologetics are rather sketchy. He brings God down to a human level, and tries to see him "from below" in a carnal way. Each time he does this, he stumbles over what men have made of God and His commandments through the centuries. So much so that it is difficult to discuss religion with him. He tells me that "Genghis Khan, who assassinated five million people, did not perish for it, because he killed them in the name of the God of love." The latest news, which he has told me with a sort of indifference, is that he is going blind because he has a cataract and absolutely refuses to have surgery for it!

My mother is very ill. She is beginning to suffer, and her doctors are most pessimistic. I write her very often, especially about the Gospel. Last week she received Communion and we are going to ask the Father Superior of my former school to go and see her.

Pierrette, at present, doesn't feel at all disposed to consider religion objectively. Yet I should love to have her give Veronica the basics of religious instruction.

And you, little brother, in ten days you will be a priest. Can you tell me about your Ordination, and at what time you will become a priest? And when you will celebrate your first Mass? I will be united with you. I have the rite of Ordination in my missal.

Your definition of a priest is very good: Jesus crucified! "But as for me, God forbid that I should glory in anything but the cross of Our Lord Jesus Christ." You are orientating your entire life toward the Passion of Christ.

As for me, I feel called to a special devotion to the Blessed Virgin Mary. If I could put it this way, I have the impression that she is more accessible to me, and I never feel the effects of prayer more than when I recite a Hail Mary.

Little brother, I imagine you must be overflowing with joy. Your last letter was a hymn of love and thanksgiving. As for me, I'm more like a snail, crawling along the path of faith, stumbling at every third step and moaning and groaning over each obstacle to be overcome. But could it be that I am better off this way? I used to move along with facility, as if I were being carried by another. Now, I am given a little bit of the cross to carry, and I make a face over it.

Dear little brother, I'll write again for your Ordination. I remain united with you.

> Your brother Jacques, who
> embraces you in Christ Jesus.

Jacques' friend Brother Thomas has just been ordained a priest.

*Wednesday, May 30, 1956*

Dear little brother,

You're a priest! I was very united with you on Saturday May 26, but so far away, alas, in the solitude of my cell. I would love to have been able to come and be present at your First Mass with your family, and receive Communion from your hands. I was very touched that you offered your private Mass on Monday the 28th for my intentions and those of my family. Where do you get so much love and strength from, little brother?

I feel like a human wreck right now, with so little courage and ardor, "for my days have vanished like smoke, and my skin cleaves to my bones." But you are right, little brother, this long period of dryness is certainly more profitable for my spiritual growth. Only it's hard, Lord! "I am not at ease, nor am I quiet; I have no rest; but trouble comes" (Job 3:26), and being abandoned leaves me disconcerted. I feel forsaken, left to myself, and I see to my horror that all I thought was behind me, all I believed was over and done with, is standing there at the threshold of my soul. The same wicked thoughts, as venomous as before my conversion, assail me with the same force, seducing my spirit, and I need all the strength I possess to fend them off. I have the impression that, having reached such a degree of degradation, I am now back at the point where I was when I formerly yielded to these temptations. It is as if there were a curve, starting at the lowest point of moral degeneration and rising to a given height. Along this curve my spirit moves, passing from the blackest thoughts to the most delicate sentiments.

Actually, I believe that I really will be preserved from too gross temptations. They are doubtless necessary for humility, otherwise one might settle down into an easy somnolence. It is terrible to know that one is doing evil, and to go on doing it just the same. "Sin has seduced me and caused me to die because of the law." I have never understood this word of St. Paul so well as at this moment: "I will show you what you must suffer for My name."

But I have so little confidence in myself, little brother, I know so well that I have no will power and am easily seduced, that I often live in a sort of fog which hides reality from me, and can see nothing but the object of my desires — so much so that if the Lord did not preserve me from too gross temptations... "Ask, and it will be given to you. . . how much more will your Father in heaven give good things to those who ask Him."

I believe that in my last letter I spoke to you of my family. There is nothing new in the last fifteen days. My mother is very ill and suffers a great deal. She cannot take morphine and holds up only because of her vitality. I asked my sister to go and look for the former director of St. Erembert, so that he might administer the last sacraments to her. As of now, I think he has already gone to her. As for my father, he is crushed!

Dear little brother, good-bye for now. It goes without saying that I am united with you each morning, at the hours you indicated to me. Ordinarily I begin my prayers at about 7:45.

I embrace you with all my heart in Christ, and will write soon.

Jacques

*Friday, June 8, 1956*

Dear little brother,

I'm writing just a line to let you know of my great loss and grief. My mother died yesterday morning at dawn. Since the evening before she had been in a coma, and after a few hours her exhausted heart stopped. It is hard, little brother, and I believe that I cannot take in the depth of the loss fully as yet. She died as a Christian. Unfortunately she was unable to receive Communion, being unconscious, but she had received the sacred Host shortly before. "Happy those who die in the Lord." The funeral Mass will take place tomorrow at Vesinet at nine in the morning. Alas, there's no question of my going. But on Wednesday morning the chaplain is going to offer Mass for her at seven. Will you unite with us, little brother?

It was a great strain waiting from one day to the next to receive the bad news. Now that it has happened, I am helpless and exhausted, as if a mountain had just fallen upon me.[3] "O sweet Jesus, grant her eternal rest, and let perpetual light shine upon her."

Good-bye, little brother, I embrace you in Christ Jesus.

Jacques

In the lines which follow, as in many others elsewhere, we can gauge the futile cruelty of our penal system. That society needs to be protected, that the guilty need to be punished, we agree, but not at the price of the moral degeneration of the condemned.

Do we who are "free" ever think of this army of living dead buried in our prisons, who for the most part will go out one day, not regenerated but forever destroyed? Do we have the right to accept this?

*Monday, August 26, 1956*

Dear little brother,

It's ages since I've written to you — soon it will be two months! It's not that I didn't want to. Very often I was ready to write, but when I picked up my pen I couldn't manage two words. I don't know if it is because of my general state, but for almost three months now, things have not gone well with me. I feel tired and spiritless, even a little obstinate, especially since my mother's death. When she was living, I had the strength to struggle, feeling that she was with me, supporting me. Now, there is a kind of lassitude and discouragement which make

---

[3] With his mother's death, there began for Jacques a period of physical and moral exhaustion.

me view everything with indifference. I think it's time for me to leave here.

You see, what is most depressing is the perpetual inaction and solitude. How many hours pass by as I sit in a corner with nothing to do but look at the wall! [Jacques had spent almost three years in absolute solitude, silence and inaction.] One ends by becoming totally unbalanced, and this imbalance is inevitably destructive. There is a kind of self-defense reflex which leads one to envisage reprisal in ways that have nothing of the Gospel about them. There is no way out, and even if this sentiment is a passing one, I believe there is still time for it to make its lasting mark on my soul. The reprisal of a beast!

You would have to be here to understand how disastrous incarceration can be for a person. With time, a man may acquire the external appearance of submission, but all the while a frightful gangrene is spreading in his soul. He is like a wildcat watching for one false step on the part of his trainer, and ready to leap. But don't be too frightened, little brother, I have already gone through other crises like this one, and come out of them.

Some time ago the chaplain told me you had written him, confiding to him your hope of being able to visit me. I don't think this would be easy to manage, however, since I am under "maximum security" and I'm very much afraid they would not want to make an exception to the rule. I suppose the chaplain has replied to you. My lawyer, Baudet, will probably come to pay you a visit one of these months at Pierre-qui-Vire. He is planning on going there for a retreat. At present he is in Jerusalem for a few more days and I suppose he must be enjoying it.

As to my case, it is drawing to a close. I think my trial will come up in February or March if nothing new occurs. Three years of detention is a long time! Especially in view of the results we can expect.

Little brother, I received your last letter as well as your schedule of duties. You have very full days and nights! I try to imagine myself in your place, and don't think I could stand such a regime for very long. It's already hard enough to keep calm here… In fact, eight days ago I was penalized for the first time and sent to the dungeon for a few days. Physically I didn't stand up under it very well, and was pretty drained when I got back here. My division and cell were changed and I have been transferred to the first division, cell 91 (this is my address now).

Pierrette always comes faithfully to visit me. She seems to have recovered her balance, but the poor girl is quite disturbed nonetheless. Her future is rather somber, and I'm always afraid that some day she will fall into the blackest despair. What misfortune that I have this burden to carry also. Lord, what a cross You have given me to carry!

All the same, I'm keeping up my spirits pretty well. Everything will work out in the end. But it will take a long time, and I have so little confidence in myself that, if I weren't specially protected, I fear I'd once more choose "the broad road." Well, little brother, I'm going to pull myself together, and I'm sure my next letter will be more cheerful. I'll write soon. I leave you, and embrace you in Christ Jesus.

Jacques

The illness which was purifying Jacques did not abate. But a continual protection was assured him, and this did not abate either. At the same time, he was constantly being taught: "This is God's will for me…" Can we measure the docility to the Holy Spirit which was required, to be able, in such a state, in the prime of life and with so black a future hanging over him, to write about these things and live them? A presentiment — and Jacques knew where it came from — already warned him, so to speak, of the way his case would go.

*The Nativity of the Virgin Mary, September 8, 1956*

Dear little brother,

I received your long, kind letter and it did me much good. Every time I read one of your letters, I see my unworthiness and weakness a little more clearly. I'm always afraid that you'll be disappointed in me on account of my tepidity and my unchristian complaints, you who are "consumed with zeal for the Father's house." I am happy that I shall see you, but don't expect marvels. I'm nothing but an apathetic sinner who is struggling very feebly against his bad conscience.

As to your visit, of course whatever day and time is best for you will be best for me too. You know I haven't received very many visits since my mother's death — one or two a month. Only, we shall have to conform to current regulations, which limit the use of the parlors as follows: Mondays, Wednesdays and Fridays from one to three in the afternoon. Only a half-hour is permitted. We can't see each other freely. Each parlor consists of a little wooden cell divided by a double grille with an empty space between of about a yard. It's not easy to see each other through this, and of course nothing can be passed through. Therefore, without a special dispensation, it would be impossible for me to receive Communion from you. I truly hope that with the chaplain's help we will be able to arrange it. But I know so well the rigidity of the regulations!

As for coming in the morning, it would be impossible, unless of course by special dispensation. Normally the earliest you could come would be one o'clock. We may be able to succeed in having our visit in the lawyer's parlor; there we would be able to talk freely without any hindrance.

You must be excited at the thought of seeing places you loved after such a long absence, and persons so dear to you.[4] There is something poignant about the thought that you are going to go out for the last time, and that many long years await you within the confines of your abbey, years filled with sacrifices, offerings, and prayers! If only I had half your zeal!

Good-bye, little brother. I leave you, and embrace you in Christ Jesus.

Jacques

---

[4] Jacques is referring to Father Thomas's brief visit to his family in Saint-Germain-en-Laye.

*Monday, November 12, 1956*

Dear little brother,

It seems an eternity since I have written you. Each day I begin to write, but I feel so empty, so remote, that I can't put two words together. Besides, I'm navigating in the most sordid waters of family interests and claims [since the death of his mother]. I believe that as far as I am concerned it would be presumptuous to think of anything whatsoever, but I do have to watch out for the future of my daughter. This business leaves me keyed up and, I admit, very mundane. For some time I have been living in "the real world," as if my fate were not what it is. I have never experienced such an inner struggle between the permanent desire to live according to God's will and the temptations and rebellion stirred up by three years in a cell. It's a case of the angel and the beast! But you know, since I've been here I've always had the very strong impression of being the object of continual protection, in spite of my outbursts of rebellion. I think that outside I did not have the grace, but that the divine will awaited me here in order to begin to build a life such as I could not have lived before. I often wonder about the freedom that is left to us. Didn't Christ say, "Father, I have lost none of those whom You gave Me"? I feel as if I were being carried along by invisible stretcher-bearers. I retain a sense of freedom but yet I am being firmly supported, and on the right road.

And so, little brother, as you told me, it is not our feelings that matter, but our will. I suppose this holds for good as well as for evil. At present I must say I have no great inclination to pray. I feel empty and hollow and can't stop my thoughts from travelling beyond the bars. The strange thing is that I've never before had such a strong feeling of my unworthiness and bad will...

Little brother, I was very glad to see you, and now I can picture you much more clearly than in the past. Alas, your face will always be crisscrossed for me with prison grilles. Prisoner of men, but also the prisoner of Christ.

Good-bye, little brother. I promise to write more regularly.

Jacques

*Friday, December 21, 1956*

Dear little brother,

In four days it will be Christmas! I should love to be able to spend the Christmas feasts with you. Your beautiful Offices must make the soul rise of its own accord in lightness and joy. Alas, as far as Offices go, I shall not even have my usual Mass, as the chaplain won't be here next week. I shall read it in my cell, but, O God, how monotonous to recite the sacred texts in almost complete darkness and in front of a wall. But as you told me, it is not joy that matters, but the effort of the will. All the same I hope this will be my last Christmas here. Baudet wants me to make a second appeal,[5] which would mean that the hearing would not take place until eighteen months from now, but acting on the advice of my family, and to my great relief, we are stopping the payments and I think my case will be judged around February. I would prefer to lance the abscess rather than drag on here for the sake of a result which is so uncertain. Besides, the family is beginning to lose interest in the whole affair, and before long I shall find myself all alone.

Pierrette is always the same. She comes to see me every Saturday with absolute regularity. Morally and physically, she is not very strong, always tired and somewhat bitter. Now I am able to give her a little material help, which is a very good thing.

My little girl is growing fast, and wrote me a very nice letter with her mother's help. Poor little girl! I should so love to see her! Well, some day...

Dear little brother, have a good Christmas, in the joy of peace rediscovered, and may the Lord fill you with His gifts on this night of reconciliation. I suppose your very strict rule is somewhat relaxed on Christmas. Wasn't it the Poor Man of Assisi who said that at Christmas, if even the walls could eat meat, we should give it to them?

Good-bye, little brother. I embrace you with all my heart in Christ.

Jacques

---

[5] A second appeal with fresh information.

*Thursday, February 1, 1957*

Dear little brother,

I started two letters to you but couldn't finish them, I have been so nervous and preoccupied about my upcoming appearance in court. We should have made an appeal, but in view of the slight enthusiasm this decision met with in my family, I preferred to give it up, and now the trial will probably take place during the first two weeks of March. When all is said and done, I'd rather be finished with this very painful business at once, especially since the result can no longer be changed. A little sooner or a little later! […]

Baudet would certainly have preferred to postpone everything for another year, but all things considered, I don't believe this would have made much difference. So there it is, little brother. I'm going to have to render an account to men for what I have done. I don't expect much from human mercy. I'm simply anticipating the worst. The most terrible thing about it is that these judgments are always more or less influenced by the changing conditions of the times, by similar cases, by the need to make an example of someone, and so forth. It seems somehow as if a person is being judged not for definite actions, classified in their respective categories, but rather as a symbol of a category of individuals who must be punished, and that this punishment is being concretized in one guilty man. Well, it's always been this way.

Pierrette comes to see me every Saturday. Materially she is coping a little better, especially since I have been able to help her more substantially. But morally things are not going well. As for my own moral state, I have to admit that for a very long time I have been drifting in a sort of lassitude which makes me view everything with indifference.

To keep my mind occupied, I'm studying English every day, and mineralogy, which I'm mad about. I don't read much else, except for a few magazines and religious books. I'm going to try to get hold of the new book on *The Living Bible* which discusses miraculous facts as seen by science. It's interesting, because instead of down-playing miracles, science confirms them. Something for all the Thomases, who want to put their fingers in the wounds!

Dear little brother, I didn't mean to leave you without news for such a long time, but I always feel so empty, or else so worked up, that I hardly know what I am doing or thinking.

Good-bye for now, little brother! Peace be with you always, and may you always rejoice in Christ crucified.

Your brother Jacques, who embraces you in Christ.

*Monday, March 4, 1957*

Dear little brother,

I received your letter and the photos, which gave me much pleasure. Thank you. I have placed them in my Missal with the little note about the liturgical days which are special to you. The date of the trial is set for April 3rd, and the verdict will probably not be given before the 5th or 6th (my birthday!). Three or four very painful days. Baudet, who must have written you, is not very hopeful, I believe. Present circumstances are not too favorable because of some recent very unpleasant cases, and he is a bit fearful that they will want to make an example of me. As for me, I'm not thinking about it. All these trials are theatrical, with much publicity, and the outcome is often "weird". In a way I am glad to get on with it, so as to be relieved of this rest cure. May God's will be done!

As to our future correspondence, as long as I am here I can write you freely. After that, I don't know how it will be, but I hope to get the necessary permission, perhaps not at once, but a little later on.

Pierrette still comes to see me regularly, but she is growing more and more rebellious and bitter, prepared for anything and with no illusions. The publicity of the trial will be very painful for her. Her boss is talking about giving her a vacation for the month of April, but she is wondering if, instead, she will be fired! All this is very difficult, and the company is much at fault. I'm not too sure how to advise her.

It is certain that her future is very dark and that she and Veronica will both have a heavy cross to carry. Only faith can save them, but she doesn't want to hear it spoken of, and I am so weak and so lacking in "charity" that I am not in a good position to make her understand where her salvation lies. We come from a proud and violent race.

Wednesday, I shall go to Mass, the first time in fifteen days, since the chaplain was away last week. It is a good opportunity for me to recall that we are but dust and ashes, and that I shall be returning to dust sooner than I had expected! I believe the trial will be very difficult, especially for my father, who bears part of the moral responsibility, which he doesn't yet realize. I have advised Pierrette to stay away from the trial as far as possible; her testimony would not be of great importance.

I am eager for next month. Dear little brother, I think I need a great deal of faith and love. "If I have not charity, I am like a clashing cymbal." — "Charity believes all, hopes all, endures all. Charity will never pass away." This is the season when Christians who had committed grave faults used to undergo public penance; then they were driven out of the church until Holy Thursday, the day when they obtained their reconciliation through their works of penance. It is the same for me. I must confess my faults (which I naturally shall not enjoy), then receive a heavy penance (utterly repugnant to me, humanly speaking) and await general forgiveness (which my pride would refuse).

Dear little brother, good-bye. I'll write you before the end of the month. On the first day of the trial, April 3rd, I will go to Mass. I embrace you in Christ.

Your brother,
Jacques

*Monday, April 1, 1957*

Dear little brother,

"But I am a worm and no man, the disgrace of men and the scorn of the people." When you receive this letter, I shall be undergoing judgment. Pray for me, little brother, for it is going to be very hard, not only for me but for the whole family. Then, may God's will be done… "They opened their jaws against me, like a lion raging and roaring." The verdict will be rendered on Tuesday April 9th, or at the earliest, Saturday April 6th. I shall hear about it from all sides, and I, who am somewhat impressionable, am wondering how I will react. At the moment, I feel strangely calm, but I don't think this will last. It is the calm that goes before the storm. If only I can answer the questions they ask correctly, and do not start to blabber, as most accused men do. The hardest thing is that it is practically impossible to act natural, and that one ends up by giving a false impression. May the Lord help me and protect me. "Do not withdraw from me, for distress is upon me, and I have no one to help me."

Good-bye, little brother. I embrace you in Christ.

Jacques

# CHAPTER 8

# THE TRIAL

On Wednesday, April 3, 1957, the trial opened. It continued until Saturday, April 6th, and ended with Jacques Fesch's condemnation to death.

Most of the journalists present made no secret of their feelings, and believed, after his lawyer's defense, that Fesch's life would be spared. While the court and jury deliberated, news reporters gathered around a microphone during an early evening broadcast and gave their opinions on the case. Only one thought the death penalty justified.

During the four days of the hearings the atmosphere of a major trial hung over the courtroom, that atmosphere which catches the accused unaware, paralyzes him — unless he is a good actor — and prevents him from acting normally and showing himself as he is.

A climate of melodrama reigned in the courtroom. Each person had a part to play. Floriot and Sudaka, counsels for the prosecution, and Paul Baudet, counsel for the defense, confronted one another in a struggle in which a show of self-importance was not lacking.

In reality the fight was unequal. On the one side, every means at the disposal of the law was used with ferocity. On the other, moderation and truth were stressed, and a kind of dignity which still did not exclude emotion and the grimness of an unyielding defense.

The crowd too played its part, by its mere presence in the packed room, its eagerness for raw emotion, and its undisguised reactions.

Jacques Fesch had no desire to play the actor. He wanted to act as naturally as possible. His emotion was none the less real but was manifested only by a tightening in the throat which prevented him from making a deeply moving appeal, and by a play of facial muscles which could be seen only by those near him. Moreover, in addition to his concern for his own fate, Jacques was much preoccupied with that of his two accomplices. He wanted them to be cleared at all costs.

His judges completely misunderstood his attitude. Because he refrained from the unsavory playacting so common in courtrooms, they thought him cynical, unfeeling, and proud.

When the president questioned him, he answered:

> Everything that happened was independent of my will. I no longer know how I attacked the money-changer. As for the policeman, he was nothing but a vague form in front of me. I was overcome with terror. My firing on him came from my subconscious. It was inevitable, a thing over which I had no control.

They did not believe him.

His father, called as a witness, could only repeat on several occasions: "I tell you, my son is a poor type. He is retarded."

Obviously the man had been drinking. This was the usual thing for him, but perhaps today it was also motivated by the need to muster up his courage. His appearance in a black shirt and shabby suit seemed so strange that people thought it had been staged by the defense.

No importance was attached to his bizarre testimony, which in the end failed to bring Jacques Fesch the help he might have hoped for. And Baudet had to limit himself to concluding, in view of its inadequacy, "I would certainly not be so cruel as to make a point of this, but I should like the court to consider the kind of father the man I am defending here had."

The majority of other witnesses tried to demonstrate that Jacques Fesch's crimes were premeditated, and that he carried them out in cold blood. They brought out the fact that, unknown to his father, he had gone to the latter's house in Anjou looking for a gun, had loaded it before the assault, and had also taken a hammer with him. In addition, during the pursuit after the assault he had picked up the handker-chief he had dropped, had gone up to the fifth floor of a building and then descended calmly to allay suspicion. He had killed the officer with a single bullet aimed straight at his heart,[1] and had fired again at another pursuer. It would be difficult to counter all these charges.

The counsel for the plaintiff fought methodically for the condemnation of the accused, and the prosecuting attorney demanded the death penalty. The final answer of the counsel for the defense follows:

> You have portrayed an aggressor [Baudet was addressing the counsel for the plaintiff] who planned everything in advance. Do you really believe that what happened was done with the deliberate intention of murder, the charge against my client today? Do you really think he set out to kill the policeman? What reason could he have had to hate this man? He was caught by circumstances in a tragic situation which led him to act, momentarily, like a criminal. He acted in panic, he fired in terror of his pursuers. Does he really deserve to be handed over to death? Is the death the people are clamoring for really proportionate to what he has done? Yesterday, a death occurred through the weakness of a human will betrayed by animal instinct. Tomorrow, on the scaffold, it will be a death determined by the cold intransigence of your will. Yesterday, it was an unexpected death, perpetrated in circumstances of utter desperation. Tomorrow, it will be a death that has been carefully prepared. They will cut carefully through his shirt in order to sever his neck. No! No crime merits another crime![2]

---

[1] Unfortunately the lawyer did not mention that Jacques Fesch was very near-sighted. His military record shows that his vision was 2/10 and 5/10; he was not permitted to use firearms. At the moment of the tragedy, he was not wearing glasses

[2] Twenty years before Paul Baudet's time, Moro-Giafferi had written: "Capital punishment presupposes an infallible judge."

We know the answer of the court and the jury: Jacques Fesch was condemned to death. His two companions were acquitted. Standing erect, Jacques received the verdict in silence. It was his twenty-seventh birthday.

# CHAPTER 9

# JACQUES' REFLECTIONS ON HIS TRIAL

Two months after his condemnation to death, Jacques Fesch responded to a request to describe his reactions and reflections during and after his trial.

Can you explain your actions?
Why did you commit the murder?
Did you see the policeman?
Did you understand his warning?

One prepares for a trial without too many illusions, and in addition, time has done its work. It has been such a long time! As far as I was concerned, and without overlooking the gravity of my case, there was such an incoherence in all my actions that I hoped things would work themselves out naturally. Was I willing to be judged? Frankly, no. I felt exhausted and knew beyond all doubt that I would have to pay for this involuntary murder as for an unforgivable crime, in order that an example might be made of me. An example... what a monstrosity! As if one man should pay the price for all future hypothetical crimes... And then I passed through varying states of mind, of submission and rebellion, right up to the great day. Whether one wishes it or not, three years in a cell do a fair job of completely destroying one's vitality and illusions. One feels weariness, a tendency to be fatalistic, and also irritation at all this rehashing of things after three years. It's quibbling. Why, at such and such a time, on such and such a day, were you there, and why... ? Oh forget it! I know I shouldn't have gone there, but there I was. Let them club me if they want, but don't let them wear me out any longer going over and over this affair. There's a little of this feeling, and a little anguish too.

One wonders what attitude one should assume. It's so important! Too many tears? A coward. Not enough tears? A cynic. One also has to plan very carefully what one is going to say. The people have power, and there are so many of them. And how precarious it all is! They are impressionable, quickly excited, ready to pounce on you for the least word that could be taken in more than one sense. I felt keyed up the first day; after that, no.

Should I add this? It may be pride, but I felt a bit of scorn for these men who were playing with the life of a fellowman without any risk to themselves, and who would be willing to belie the facts deliberately in order to meet the demands of their professional pride or interests. As if the truth were not already tragic enough!

Some witnesses who were called up spoke impressively at first of their long experience, then gave their opinions on what "must" have happened. Their main object was to demolish the presentation of the accused in the eyes of the jury. It is impossible to describe the dissembling, the all too obviously staged air of frankness. They then went on to say: "In spite of my knowledge of crimes and my long experience, I have been deeply disturbed by the monstrosity of these acts. I had expected to see a man bowed down under the weight of his guilt. But no, Jacques Fesch looks calm to me, sure of himself. He is the picture of disdainful superiority; he is unusually cold-blooded. . ." Superiority! with his face streaming blood and bruised with blows?[1] "Oh, the cold-bloodedness!" How they kept stressing it!

Then came the *curriculum vitae*, my life history. They brought up everything prejudicial to the accused and omitted all the rest. A stream of witnesses followed, honest men I am convinced, who told what they saw or thought they saw. Their testimonies were contradictory, but remained the same in principle. In the beginning, when I heard them talk about my imperturbable "cold-blooded-ness" I was angry, thinking they were trying to take revenge on me. But as the

---

[1] Consequences of his arrest.

trial continued, I realized that they were certainly sincere. The private parties then filed through, men without rancor who also reported what they had seen. One felt that the condemnation of the accused did not interest them, that it was merely a matter of grievances and vested interests... What side comedies there were! One witness accused another of giving false testimony in order to establish the guilt of one of the accused men, who, once condemned, should himself have wrongs to avenge. Protestations... They spoke a great deal about honor, integrity... It had a false ring. The president maintained a fatherly air, but whether consciously or not, tended to favor the prosecution. Two days later, some lawyers came to appeal for the defense. They endeavored to carry their point with the people. "They are just doing their job" was the reaction — honest for some, bitter for others. The lawyers were addressing their plea to the one who had the best chance of obtaining capital punishment, and paying no attention to whether the evidence was true or false. At that moment I had a clear impression that the whole trial had been slanted in advance.

The final effort of the pack before the kill. Four lawyers succeeding each other for hours on end, and hammering on the minds of the jurors with the words: killer, killer, killer... The first was hard but not insistent; and not very convincing. The second was intent upon emphasizing the sufferings of the victim and drawing the logical conclusions. As for the third: a legal mind at work, pouring out methodical and destructive fury for two hours.

To sum up, actions which had taken place within two or three minutes were dissected, analyzed, and discussed for four days.

And now that I find myself here in my cell once more, two months later, having had time to appreciate my situation and to take it in better, you ask me what I think about the judgment? I have questioned my conscience: what do you think? what do you feel? how do you assess the situation?

Guilty, yes. I committed this assault, under the influence of the character which had been shaped for me by the circumstances of my life, but I did not will it. I have not tried to dodge my responsibilities and I have always been willing to pay for what my crimes deserved.

The murder? Guilty, yes. It is right and just that I should pay the price for a crime which resulted from a previous criminal action. What can I say? That I simply should not have fired? Impossible. I can no longer even remember what happened. And if I had been able to see the face of this man, fallen and mortally wounded, what image would have haunted me? Impossible question again. It was night time... Remember Rousseau's mandarin.[2]

The reckless drunken driver who kills a passerby could just as well be condemned to death. And then, there are other opinions. One says, "All the same, you did assault a money-changer, you killed a policeman, and you fired on the crowd. Can't you put yourself in their place?" Of course, but these are facts. Does God judge facts?

The social usefulness of capital punishment is understandable, and yet it offends the consciences of those involved. A person may think, "Condemned to death in France, yes... but if it were somewhere else?" Then he remembers all the countries where capital punishment is no longer allowed. This illustrates the weakness of human institutions, as Pascal would say.

And further, one thinks, doesn't the social structure have a bit of responsibility for all that happened? It is there to protect people, granted, but it is also there to help those who have perhaps received less than others. The character without mercy professes to be shocked. He is not prone to very generous attitudes.

There is only one thing left to do: ignore all this hatred, and search within and without for the One who waits unwearyingly for the bruised and desperate soul, to give him a treasure denied to the world. . . To encounter Christ, whose voice falls clearer perhaps in the solitude of a cell than elsewhere: "And others will lead you where you do not want to go..."

But I'm human, and I protest, "Lord, take away Your hand, for I am smothering." —

---

[2] An allusion to this paradox attributed to Rousseau: "If all you had to do in order to become the wealthy heir of a man you never saw, never heard of, and who lived at the farthest extremity of China — if all you had to do to cause his death was to push a button, which of us would not push the button?"

"And I, who did nothing, did I not endure the nails and the thorns?"

Then I reply impulsively, "But You were God." —

"God, yes, but it was My flesh that was crucified."

And then these words come to mind, so moving and so full of meaning for the man who suffers:

"Father, take this chalice from Me..."

and,

"Woman, I don't know what you are saying, I do not know the man."

At the last, in the light of faith, I accept the cross, which gradually becomes so light I scarcely feel it. I offer up my suffering, the injustices done to me. I love those who strike me, and I know that one day I shall hear these words, like the good thief on the cross,

"Amen I say to you, this day you will be with Me in paradise."

# CHAPTER 10

# THE HOUR OF DARKNESS

For Jacques, the death sentence fell like a premature death in its own right. Doubtless he still had his hopes. Everyone who lives has hope. But at the same time, he had no illusions.

A new stage in his life was beginning. The man was crushed, but mysteriously God continued His work. The man was worn down, but not broken. He was without strength, but not abandoned.

Hope was no more than a smoking wick, but a light dawned and accompanied him on his journey. Jacques, docile, allowed himself to be drawn along in its wake. He sounded the depths of human poverty and misery and at the same time discovered that he had never been less alone.

For the moment his spiritual journey, with its progressive ascent, seemed to have come to a halt. After his condemnation his soul was troubled ("My soul is troubled even unto death…"), but soon, and without any "merit" on his part, there would come the radiance of light, strength, and joy, and it would last to the very end.

FIRST LETTER AFTER THE VERDICT:

*Saturday, April 27, 1957*

Dear little brother,

"Draw near to Him, the living stone, rejected by men but chosen and honored by God." Have I perhaps come to the end of my life? A very short life, not too full, but clotted with evil, tears and blood. I haven't much to be proud of! It is true that the Lord loves to choose what is feeble and rejected, in order to show that it is by His grace, acting through our weakness, that we are saved.

The only thing I can glory in is my trials, sufferings, and crosses, provided I accept them whole-heartedly and offer them to our Lord in reparation for my sins. That is why the Apostle said, "I glory in nothing but the cross of our Lord." Only, my nature is so evil that I cannot bring myself to accept so painful a lot, and I have settled for a rather fatalistic resignation, which is very far from what Christ asks of me.

In truth, little brother, I have done much evil in this world, and I deserve to be condemned with the damned. O, that I may hear on the day of my judgment: "Jacques, God the Father, whose compassion is infinitely greater than your sins, will pity you deeply and will grant you many graces."

For the moment, I am not in the state of soul my situation calls for. I murmur from time to time against the Lord's shackles, wishing that the heavy hand which has so long weighed upon me might relax its pressure a little. I am like a stubborn horse held in check by an inflexible bit, rearing up in its effort to return to the camps of sinners. My will is extremely weak, and I do not share as I should in this work of resurrection willed by the Savior. Like a child that cannot walk alone without falling, if the Lord does not fill me with graces and overcome my will I shall fall back again. It is the hour of darkness, little brother. The devil is prowling around me "like a roaring lion" on the lookout for his prey. Well he knows he can snatch me unless spiritual help comes to rescue me from his jaws.

[…]

I embrace you in the risen Christ.

Jacques

*Wednesday, June 5, 1957*

Dear little brother,

Baudet mailed your beautiful letter to me already eight days ago. Forgive me for writing you so seldom, when your love never fails me. I often feel profoundly ungrateful toward the Lord, who has entrusted my salvation in some part to you, and ungrateful to you, whose charity and patience are marked with a faithfulness unknown to the world.

Now, you see, the road I am following is full of ruts, and I have to admit that most of the time I'm walking in trenches rather than on smooth ground. I'm often weary and indifferent to everything. Or else I'm grinding my teeth, and my soul is invaded by the infernal racket of little devils who stir up dreams and ideas that have nothing in common with the Gospel.

You are right, little brother, when you say, "I know Satan is prowling around you..." How he must gloat at the sight of my impressionable soul, which can't possibly rise above itself without the help of extraordinary divine gifts. I have no strength, I lack the charity which would soften my heart, and I don't possess the gift of wisdom; but I believe that at this painful time the Lord has given me that gift of understanding "which enlightens us with its keen rays, and gives us certitude regarding the true meaning of the Word of God."

Despite all my rebellion and lack of zeal and enthusiasm for a life of communion with God, I know with absolute certainty that I am surrounded by grace and love and that the Lord wants to save me in spite of myself. *Fiat*, Lord! You know me, and You know that I am incapable of saving myself without Your constant help. But this will of mine which says *Fiat* today will say tomorrow, "Take Your hand away from me — for I am suffocating."

There's still a good deal of rancor in my soul, which of course comes from pride and leads me to do things I regret. Do you know, sometimes I think, in good faith and with horror, that the only way I can be saved is perhaps not to be saved in the human sense of the word? Confidence, confidence, little brother!

Yes, indeed, you may write to me as often as you like, to the Santé prison. There are no restrictions on this score.

Recently I saw Pierrette. She is very happy because a long and excellent article of Marcelle Auclair's has just appeared in *Marie-Claire*. It seems it is deeply moving. I should so much like to read it, but we are not allowed to see this kind of magazine. I am always very united with Pierrette, but perhaps not with all the charity I should have. I get worked up easily, and my own problems blind me to those of others.

As for Baudet, you are perfectly right. It would be wrong and also unfair to reproach him, no matter what happens. At first I was somewhat annoyed, because I had come to that trial in good faith, and everything that took place there was so artificial and theatrical that I almost wanted to respond in the same spirit. When I heard Baudet pleading my cause, saying only the exact truth without prevarication, even without insistence, and when I observed the reaction of the other side, which had just finished serving up more or less bizarre and fantastic accounts, I wished that my lawyer had charged into them headlong and demolished their arguments with their own weapons.

I expect to hear the result of the final appeal in eight or ten days. I will let you know right away what happens, but I'm almost sure it will be rejected. I doubt whether you should offer such a painful Mass, not knowing whether I am dead or alive. I'll write you the day when my lawyer is summoned to the President of the Republic. After that there will be three or four days without any information, and then as soon as the result is known Baudet will send you a telegram. A few more months of relative calm will follow...

In three days it will be Pentecost, little brother. May the Lord make me understand a little more deeply the wonder of His love. If I could make a wish, it would be that I might be able to appreciate more completely the fact that all that is happening comes from His mercy, and that if I am to be rejected and discarded by men it is because the Lord wants to give me the greatest of all goods: glory in the risen Christ. As I wrote you, I feel this, but I do not realize all its importance and grandeur. Were I brutally enlightened, as the dead must be, I would know how wretched and ungrateful I am! "If you knew the gift that is given you this day…" But, I don't know it yet — the flesh is so miserable, the spirit so weak! I believe if I could grasp God's thought, and if it were transmitted to me orally, this is what I would hear: "What hopeless corruption! He's like a straw! No sooner does he abandon himself to Me than he falls back again, wallowing in his filth and abjection!"

What would it take to change my nature? But confidence, confidence! I admit everything, and I hope. It's up to You, Lord, to do all the work. All I am capable of is offending You.

Good-bye, little brother. I leave you with an embrace and hug in the glorified Christ. —

Jacques

The solitude is profound, time drags on endlessly. Jacques the nature-lover turns to books about animals. He writes to his mother-in-law, Madame Polack, on June 26th, 1957:

Last evening I was so bored that I read the same book through twice. I was back in Florida with the bears and the does. I really love animals and nature… I have a practical mind that likes to set up categories and sub-categories; I store up the unusual names in my memory — all this is so alive and real to me… I have never succeeded in taking seriously the things that most people consider important. They seem to me artificial and useless, above all things made by men. To study rocks, animals or plants is to come into direct contact with concrete manifestations of the divine law. Sometimes I talk like this with Baudet, and ask him why he has wasted so much of his time burdening his mind with the antiquated and obsolete details of human law. He looks at me disparagingly then, and doesn't seem to appreciate my point of view.

But am I not right? Civilization ruins everything. What kind of life do men live in our times? Tied down to their work in the stench of

a factory or a subway, when the most wretched of the ancient Gauls
could at least live in a magnificent setting and give themselves to
simple, vibrant joys! Long live our ancestors, the Gauls!

Jacques returned to the subject of his inner transformation. It annoyed him when people attributed this to a natural "human" development. To his mother-in-law, he wrote
a little later:

You see, I am often provoked, and it annoys me when people
say that the change in me is merely on the human level. I know better
than anyone what it is. Many think that I could have avoided what
happened, and that I committed crimes as a conscious, rational criminal. Now, they think, I have come to realize what I did, I regret it, and
being transformed, I want to expiate the evil. They consider this a
second stage. Not true! Rather, it is all one integrated whole. What
happened was inevitable. Its roots are much deeper and go back much
further. A person may consent to evil for years, and nothing happens.
Unknown to him, his freedom diminishes, his body weakens, and his
will becomes atrophied. The years succeed, always transmitting a
little more of their decay, until the day when evil becomes so integral
a part of that man's being that he can no longer act freely, and allows
himself to be caught and carried along in the destructive current.

It is at this point that he discovers grace. Look at the Bible,
the history of men and nations! It's always the same thing.
Time falls away and there is a solidarity between us all.

God, essentially a Father, never ceased to enlighten
His wretched child and to give him the strength to prepare
for the events which lay ahead. Less than two more weeks,
and the grace of graces would be given him — that interior voice whose manifestation we have already mentioned.
Twice, Jacques heard it mysteriously. The first time, after
one year of detention, it had urged him to conversion. The
second time, it would tell him of his approaching death

and give him the certitude of his salvation. Then, he would exult for joy! This "state" would be his for two months, up to the last morning of his life.

Here is the last letter he wrote before entering into the *joy* which was no longer of this world:

*Sunday, July 21, 1957*

Dear little brother,

There has been a strike on for six days. A total strike. And we who were already separated from the world are now in complete isolation. No more mail, no canteen, no parlor visits, no walks. Actually, I have no idea when this letter will reach you.

As you may already know, the last appeal has been refused. This was to be expected, and I'd really rather have it this way. The lawyer[1] pleaded for a long time, making some favorable points, but unfortunately they didn't have too much connection with the case in hand. However, this hearing was not completely useless. The President's secretary was there and seemed quite impressed. The only palpable conclusion brought forward was that the alleged straightforward part heretofore attributed to the association of policemen was disproved. This seems to indicate that the police have worked overtime to bring me to my present situation. Baudet will make use of this little supplementary argument. While it's not much in itself, still it will help to reinforce the others.

So there you have it. I shall have to wait till the month of October. I'm not sure what to think, and when I try to guess what the Lord's intentions may be, I end up with feelings against Him, and then I am obliged to return to more humble thoughts. I don't think I am in the right frame of mind to face eternity. I am not rebelling, but I am not accepting things any longer. Most of all, I'm exhausted, and have become somewhat indifferent. I am neither impressed nor moved,

---

[1] Celice, President of the Order of Lawyers at the Court of Appeals.

and I believe that the conclusion, whatever it may be, will find me rather apathetic. While I still have a good deal of resilience, I'm attached to the world even at this point, and since I can't change my fate, I give it all up and fall asleep, waiting for someone to wake me either down here or up above!

If only I had your zeal and your ardor! To tell the truth, I foresee a bad ending for myself. If I should appear before the Lord, I really don't see how I could justify myself. I have nothing but catastrophes to my account, sufferings as well, yes, but didn't St. Peter say, "Let no one suffer as a thief"? And if I should not appear before the Lord, I see myself more as someone full of good intentions than as a soldier of Christ. The Lord knows better than I what is best for me, and can certainly do without my advice.

I received, together with your last letter, that of the young woman you mentioned to me. What faith she has! I feel wretched indeed in comparison with you two. The joy with which the Lord enlightens you shines through all your letters. "Even if I bid them be silent, the very stones would cry out for joy…"

As for me, I am sad! Perhaps it is lack of humility that hardens my heart? I could easily become violent, and at the least contradiction I start up like a wildcat. Pride — the worst of all evils, which keeps us far from the Lord. I have much more reason to be humble, but it is just the opposite. The more I am slapped down, the more I stiffen and cling to the pride which is the source of my courage.

"Brother Leo," St. Francis said, "do you know what perfect joy is? Suppose we go back to the convent and the brother porter greets us as if we were shameless rascals, showers us with insults and blows, turns us out into the snow and leaves us without shelter or food. Well, if we have the strength of soul to think that this brother has treated us as we deserved, and if we praise the Lord for it, this will be perfect joy!" I know someone who, if he were treated like that, would not be able to resist flying at the porter.

Well, little brother, thank you for all your prayers. Baudet arranged for me to get a phone call from your mother. May the Lord reward you a hundredfold for all you have given to others and fill you here below with His joy and His love. I will write again soon. Will you thank Madame Frances for me? I pray for her, and every Wednesday I think of you near me throughout the Mass.

I leave you and embrace you in Christ.

Your brother Jacques

*Chapter 11*

# JACQUES RECEIVES THE VERDICT

The news was first brought to Jacques "humanely" by his lawyer. Considering the results of his earlier attempts, Baudet realized that a pardon was not likely to be granted to Jacques Fesch, and that the final decision would take place after the vacations. He tried to enlighten his client as tactfully as possible regarding his fate. Then God made use of this warning to work an ultimate transformation in Jacques Fesch. It was a foretaste of his entrance into the joy of the elect.

The certainty of his death was so obvious to Jacques that he had said to his lawyer, at the moment when the latter was terminating his efforts to win his pardon:

> Do everything you feel your duty requires, so that your conscience may be at peace, but I shall not be pardoned. Moreover, if I were, I should be profoundly troubled, for on two occasions God has told me, "You will receive the graces you need to die." [The first warning had been given him during the night of his conversion.]

On another occasion he told his lawyer, "God has taken possession of my little soul... the veil has been torn... If I went on living, I would never be able to stay on the heights I have now reached. Much better that I should die."

Jacques had mounted his cross. The cross of the good

thief was none the less a cross. When he spoke of his experience, his words were not pure theory:

We must first let ourselves be crucified on the cross which stands
at the entrance (of the kingdom of God, where all life, all joy is found).
If suffering and fear make us draw back, then we will not enter. It is
true that most of the time our advice is not asked (only our consent).
Otherwise, so few of those called would pass through! But with the
trial comes faith, and with faith grace, which is not given sparingly
but with profusion. The yoke becomes sweet and the sorrow is changed
into joy, and what is hidden from the eyes of men becomes luminous
for us, whom the Lord is drawing…

Do you know this word of Christ: "I thank you, Father, because
You have revealed these things to little ones, and have hidden them
from the wise"? It is true.

He then wrote these extraordinary letters which could only
be the fruit of divine light and strength. Indeed Jacques
Fesch was in direct contact with Jesus Christ. He was carried by Him and transfigured. Like Him, no one would
take his life away: he would lay it down!

FIRST LETTER OF JOY: "MY SPIRIT REJOICES IN GOD MY SAVIOR!"

*Monday, August 5, 1957*

Beloved little brother,
"My soul magnifies the Lord, and my spirit rejoices in God my
Savior." Rejoice, little brother! That which was lost has been found,
and for the second time the scales have fallen from my eyes. Truly,
the love of Christ is infinite, in having once more brought me to the
One who waits unwearyingly for those whom He loves, who is watching for my arrival as I come staggering under the weight of my cross.
All is light, warmth, and happiness once more. Think of the tremendous gift which has been restored to me!

As you wrote me — and I only understand it fully today — Jesus waits for me to believe in His love and to save myself by an act of will, sharing in the act [his decapitation] which He permits with a merciful end in view — eternal life. It is not I who am advancing toward Him, but He who once more carries me on His shoulders. I know now that everything is grace, and that it is not death I am approaching, but life. I am being saved in spite of myself. My extreme weakness led me to I know not what extravagances, and His untiring solicitude was waiting to rescue me from Satan's toils and the despair of the last hour. Now I am ready for the good fight.

The time is so short! Pray for me, little brother, that my faith does not fail. I pray above all to the Blessed Virgin, and no prayer goes without its answer. Strength is being poured into my soul in good measure, pressed down and running over. Who can describe the marvels of the Lord? I have two months ahead of me, and I know now what Jesus wants of me: total surrender of my will to His, and the positive acceptance of this penalty which had once aroused my rebellion. Just or unjust, it no longer matters. Everything is forgiven, all is superabundantly redeemed, all is confidence, now, in the infinite power of His mercy.

"See the fig tree and all the trees, when their branches grow tender and they put forth leaves, you know that summer is nigh; even so, when these things happen, you know that the kingdom of God is at hand…"

Write me, little brother, and pray for me in these last moments, I need it so much!

Your brother Jacques, who embraces you in Christ.

Jacques is constantly preoccupied about his wife's faith, or rather, the absence of it. What he sees, he wants for his family. He writes to his mother-in-law:

If Pierrette does not have faith, she will be tossed about like a straw in the wind… However I have a firm hope that she will be saved, some day or other, and that all she now lacks, and which she will have merited, will be given to her in abundance.

Understand well that it is not because of what has happened that I have life. The cross I carry so weakly in men's eyes is as glorious as that of a monk or a missionary. But how hard these things are to understand, for those who live in the world! For the onlookers, everything seems so inexplicable. […]

Only recently have I come to understand the meaning of the cross. It is both prodigious and atrocious. Prodigious, because it gives life, and atrocious because, if we do not crucify ourselves, all life is lost to us. This is a great mystery, and blessed are those who are persecuted.

On August 8, 1957, two months before his execution, he writes to his mother-in-law:

I've had my parlor visit. What suffering! Poor Pierrette is shattered… She doesn't want to go home and rest, but wants to stay near me during the coming months. I've never seen her so upset. She suffers on my account like a tigress, and above all on account of her little girl, who is beginning to sense the approaching catastrophe and who cries out for me. Poor Veronica! What ravages will these terrible events cause in her little soul?… How hard it is to accept all this devastation! […]

This is where the cross stands out in its bloody mystery. All life revolves about this wood… Don't you have the impression that whatever you plan to do in this brief hour of life that is yours, it is all marked with the seal of suffering? No escape, no more illusions. You know with certitude that what the world offers is as artificial and illusory as the ephemeral dream of a little six year old. You let yourself be invaded by despair, and you try to escape the grief that pursues and destroys you, seeking a way out that is nothing else than the rejection of the cross. There is no hope of peace or salvation outside of Christ crucified! Happy the one who understands this.

[... the next day, he continues:]

Dear Mama, [this is Madame Polack, his mother-in-law, who understands him so perfectly], you feel a tremendous need to love. Your generous heart would like to fill those whom you love with the best of yourself, and yet this treasure seems worthless to those who receive it. Who could ever satisfy this urge to always give more? One only! And that One is very close to you. He waits to give Himself to you, that you may come to recognize His face in the faces of all your dear ones.

Don't write to me of "ingratitude." If anyone finds his brother ungrateful, it is not the other's happiness he is seeking, but his own. So many trip over this stumbling block. You have to give yourself, you have to understand that on the day when you are completely detached from yourself, a torrent of grace will spring up in your heart, and joy and peace will be given you in a profusion you never thought possible. There is no salvation outside of the cross!

SECOND LETTER OF JOY: "MY HEART IS OVERFLOWING WITH LOVE."

*Thursday, August 15, 1957*

Dear little brother,

I received your last letter, which is kindness itself. Yes, you see Jesus has not even waited for me to persevere, to give me the fullness of His love. He came at once at my first sincere appeal, to relieve me of my burden. For ten days I have been living in another world, and I feel that my time of tepidity is far, far away... There is little enough time left for me to try to love Him as I ought. It is not I who love Jesus, it is Jesus who loves me. I am conscious of my total powerlessness and my misery as always. Also, I have to keep calling for help all the time, and like a generous Father the Lord strengthens me, fills me with powerful graces, and marks off my way of the cross with fragrant shrines which make me long to hasten to Him. I believe in His love, but my human confidence, which I should like to be total, is still very weak. I ought to give Him everything, and I want to achieve this...

I have asked the chaplain to bring me Communion on Wednesdays and Fridays. He will do it, and will send me a replacement during his vacation. How can I express my joy to you! Each time I receive the sacred Host my heart overflows with love, and a song of thanksgiving rises to my lips. Infinite mercy... I am saved in spite of myself. Instead of dying in vain, I can offer my life for all those whom I love. Everything comes back to the love of Jesus... I pray especially to the Blessed Virgin, to whom her Son has entrusted my salvation. No prayers give me such joy, such a spirit of communion, as the Hail Mary and the Hail Holy Queen. We must love her, little brother, she is so good. If we could only understand a fraction of the love Jesus has for us! But we are too egotistical, and we only want to see what our fleshly eyes can show us.

Today is the feast of the Assumption, probably the last great feast I shall live to see, so I have celebrated it very specially. I am glad this day is consecrated to the Virgin. It is to her that I confide my sorrows and anxieties, and I am so happy that you wrote to me, "She protects you unceasingly." It is true. When I feel alone, I need only take refuge with her, and she guards me and consoles me like a little child.

Pray much for me, little brother. In these moments which are so crucial for me, I need your love. I too pray all the time, and this is necessary if I am to drink the chalice to the dregs and offer all my sufferings, my anguish, to our beloved Lord Jesus Christ. "Not what I will, Father, but what you will."

Your brother Jacques who embraces you in Christ Jesus

Jacques, certain of the inevitable, although his plea for pardon had not yet been rejected, Jacques who saw the

truth as clearly as if he were no longer a prisoner in this
world, poured out, in the briefest of his lines, the riches of
a heart burning with the love of God. How well he knew
how to love, now!

Pierrette must find peace for herself and her little girl [he wrote
to his mother-in-law], and I am certain that at the end of life's long
trial she will find the light she has sought, and that it will fill her
beyond her capacity. People are crucifying her, too, and yet from the
beginning she never has had anything but good intentions.

All this seems unjust humanly speaking, and yet, if you could
see life as it really is in all its splendor, illuminated by the bit of
divinity which dwells in each one of us, everything would become
love and grace. I can't say I've had a very happy life, and if my faith
were limited to this world only, I should be the most miserable of
men. But at the present hour, which is so full of mortal threats, I know
that I am the most privileged of men, because what is to be given me
so far exceeds what is being taken away. Even if I were able, I would
not exchange my lot with that of an oil magnate...

This must sound strange to you, a bit exalted and tinged with
autosuggestion, and I suppose you won't attribute any great value to
it. You probably think that my imagination is running away with me,
and that I have succeeded in drugging myself because of living through
such stressful hours. There is an insuperable barrier, you see, between
those who are drawn by grace and those who are not. For the latter, all
this seems stupid, futile, or sentimental and silly, because they are
limited to human vision and human love, and faith is above all that. I
understand it all the better because I was an atheist for so long, and
sentimentality has never been my strong point...

His lawyer prays for him and has others pray. But Jacques
does not count on human help.

I just received a card from Baudet who is making a retreat at the
Carmel in Bondigne in la Sarthe. A very nice card! He seems to be

mobilizing all the holy monks of his acquaintance, and all who are in heaven as well, to "save Jacques Fesch." And Jacques Fesch will be saved, and much more too...

CHAPTER 12

# "I AM LIVING
# THROUGH MARVELOUS HOURS"

The letters which follow witness to a joy which is more intense than before, and at the same time more austere. The song which rises from them is ever truer and more personal. These last letters are the most beautiful of all. On reading them, we might say that God Himself is writing them with the hand and heart of His child, who gives his total consent to pass through the death prepared for him into the life of God. Already the heavens are opened and Fesch knows and sees. Because of what he knows and sees, he becomes joy embodied.

We need to realize that it is difficult, if not impossible, to understand a tragedy, just as it is to conceive an intense and wholly interior joy, when it is someone else's. In his three years and eight months of detention, Jacques Fesch lived in depth a unique, irreducible and incommunicable experience. A modern good thief, he is a witness and guide. His last letters, especially his last night, are gospels, that is, good news for the poor, which we all are. The first throes of an agony which was to be prolonged up to the last night are not wanting.

All of us, whatever may be our inner desolation, the gravity of our faults, or the extent of our misfortunes, are called to journey to the Promised Land. We are invited to a "passage," that is, to live our Passover, which God wills to take place in a daily progression, as He leads and sustains our efforts. The journey takes us through our daily sufferings to the land of His joy, where He Himself wipes away all tears from the sorrowful faces of men. Jacques has made this passage, has finished his course and has triumphed over death. Yes, he has indeed triumphed over death. For his part, sharing in the mystery of the communion of saints, and uniting his death with the death of Christ, Jacques has become, with Him, a savior.

<u>THIRD LETTER OF JOY: "I AM LIVING THROUGH MARVELOUS HOURS."</u>

*Tuesday, September 3, 1957*

Dear little brother,

Thank you for your good letter which I had awaited impatiently, and for your charity to me, which is "kind, patient, humble, which believes all, hopes all." Yes, little brother, I want to look neither ahead nor behind, but to remain in the present moment. I want to hold the Blessed Virgin's hand and never let go of it until she leads me to her Son.

I am living through marvelous hours, and I feel as if I had never lived any other life than the one I've been experiencing for a month now. Jesus draws me to Himself, and knowing the weakness of my soul He gives me much, while asking for so little. For each small effort that I make I receive another grace, and, in view of the shortness of the time, this ascent toward God is being achieved far more quickly than it would be for someone who still had years ahead of him.

The Blessed Virgin protects me, shows me the way I must go, and what her Son wants of me. Thus my sufferings are changed into joy, and in order to mitigate the anguish of the last moments, our good Mother makes me prefer the other world to this one.

I cannot be pardoned, little brother, and I have no illusions about it. Jesus allows this death in order to save whoever He wills to save.

At least this is all I am able to see in the present hours I am living through. "Unless the seed dies, it remains alone, but if it dies, it brings forth much fruit." We have to rejoice in the Lord's mercy and praise Him for all His works which are wonderful in our eyes.

My thoughts turn so often to my father who, alas, is going to suffer a great deal... I am offering my life for him, and I am certain that Jesus will have pity on him. When? That is still His secret. But I tremble at the thought of the sufferings which await him.

As to the question of a religious marriage [Jacques' marriage had only been civil], I have spoken with the chaplain about it and he has given it some thought. It is not possible; the authorization would be refused. On the other hand, on the practical level he doesn't think it advisable; in fact, quite the contrary. He told me of the case of a condemned man who had succeeded in obtaining the authorization and who had been pardoned. His wife could not be remarried, nor could she wait indefinitely for his possible return! What do you think about it? As for me, I would not want to do anything God did not wish me to do, and I haven't as yet the light to come to any conclusion. Anyhow, time is short. Just one more month, and this doesn't leave us time to accomplish much.

I am very happy that you think you can come here to see me. Baudet will certainly let you know the date of his summons to the President's office, but you know, after that there will be no other opportunity. We should have our visit before his summons, but I don't know whether they will authorize it for you. Not even the chaplain is allowed to enter my cell alone, so great is their confidence in me! [...]

I send you, little brother, my First Communion picture. It is the only one I possess. I wrote on it two sentences from the Gospel which I love very much. Put it in your missal too, although I know you don't need anything to remind you of me.

Good-bye, little brother. I leave you with an embrace in Christ.

Jacques

In spite of his extraordinary mystical growth, Jacques remained very human. Here are some extracts, the first of
which, written perhaps a month before his execution, ech-
oes his last and greatest human joy:

I received Veronica's little locks. What beautiful hair she has! So fine,
so blond, so soft to touch! I really feel as if I had my little girl in my
cell. Something alive of hers, that I can touch now...

But Jacques' great preoccupation was always how he could
share his faith with his family, and make them understand
the profound meaning of his sacrifice:

If you knew the seriousness of death... There is no other interpretation to give it. The nails in the hands are real, and the nails are
*accepted.* You see, I am certainly going to pass through a fearful
agony, and the preparation for this bloody procedure is horrible. If I
tremble at it, it is not because of physical fear, but because I understand better now all the purity of Christ, contrasted with my repul-
siveness. Whatever may happen to me, I shall only be saved by grace,
by grace alone...

I see from your letter that you misunderstood what I wrote you.
It is not out of weariness that I long to be gone. It is so that the Father's
will may be done; and because I accept this will with my whole heart,
I receive joy upon joy. Do you understand better now? And "He who
abandons himself to God in this way no longer has a heart of flesh
within his breast, but a globe of fire..."

To his daughter who is on a holiday:

My dear little girl,
I am very happy to get your nice little notes and I hope you will
send me some more [it is now fifteen days before his execution, and
he knows it]. I received the lovely photos of you on your holidays, and
I can see what a beautiful little girl you are, and that you are having a
good time. I know too that you received a pretty pencil case so that

you could write your papa, and that you are saying many prayers to the little Jesus and the Blessed Virgin. Papa hugs you with all his heart and he prays for you to the little Jesus, that He may protect you. Big, big kisses.

Papa

Veronica was then about six years old. I believe she has never forgotten the strange, sad, wonderful Papa whom she hardly knew. But he knew her, and loved her more than ever now.

Jacques was firmly established in profound peace. At certain moments an inexpressible joy flooded his soul. However, he still had to undergo painful interior purifications. Each of these was followed by a new ascent. The rhythm was rapid, for Heaven was near. These sufferings cannot be understood by those who have not experienced them, any more than the happiness Jacques knew. Only the mystics have lived through such spiritual adventures on this earth. They alone have described them. Jacques, in his letters, instinctively adopted their words and images. His way was authentic, and the One who guided and transformed him was none other than Jesus Christ, who is Love.

FOURTH LETTER OF JOY:
"THE LORD IS DOING GREAT THINGS WITH ME AND IN ME..."

*Wednesday, September 18, 1957*

Dear little brother,

Yesterday I received your long and very kind letter. Yes, little brother, soon, very soon, I shall enter into a blessed eternity. I have put all desires, all cares, in Jesus' hands, and since I have become docile to every inspiration, the Lord is doing great things with me and in me.

For almost two months now, I have been living days as full as if they were years. I am being pressed down, shaped, tested, in order to be found worthy to wear the white robe of the blessed. Jesus showers me with gifts. He plants a little flower of paradise in my soul, and then suddenly He takes everything away and I find myself plunged into the darkness of abandonment. "To belong to a God of light and to live in shadows, to possess in one's heart a God who is love itself and to feel oneself cold as marble... from this state come the desolations which those who have not experienced them cannot possibly understand."

I am being tried like gold in the furnace, and this in two ways: first, powerful thrusts toward the light are followed by passing darkness; second, there are more or less lengthy phases of abandonment in which all joy disappears and only aridity is left. At the moment I am being left to myself, although supported by His strength, and I am waiting patiently for the Lord to draw me to Himself once more, and to place me on a summit a little higher than the last one.

From day to day I ascend toward God, or rather, allowing His grace to act in me, I am being lifted up to that destined place from which I shall fly to paradise. I pray without ceasing, but of course during these periods of abandonment my prayer is less continual and many spontaneous acts of union are wanting to my days, so much so that I feel I am slipping a little. I assure you that I am aware of the degree of purification needed before one can be admitted to contemplation of the Lord!

Jesus is adorning my soul. He banishes the slightest evil thought, and sharpens my sensitivity and enlightens my conscience so that I can work with Him in this upbuilding. I have been in the depths of agony for nearly two months and realize clearly how impossible it is for souls to win paradise without total submission. Jesus does everything, and I let Him do it, even if it causes me some pain. I am waiting until all shall be ready for the fruit He Himself has planted to be gathered, and I lose myself in the contemplation of His infinite love.

The Blessed Virgin helps me very much, and often in a way I can feel sensibly. On the feast of her Nativity, for example, she wanted me to rejoice with her, and I spent the whole day in heaven. On the feast of Our Lady of Sorrows anguish replaced my joy, and thus I was able to spend this day with Mary at the foot of the Cross. Do you see how good our Mother is? "O Mary! blessed name that I love and venerate from the depths of my being! I attest this from my own experience: when a heart has received from heaven the precious gift of having recourse to Mary in its sorrows, dangers, and trials, this heart finds peace, rest, blessedness."

As to the religious marriage, I did not know in conscience what to think, and I asked the Blessed Virgin to take care of it... And you see! There are no more difficulties. Pierrette not only agrees, but wants with all her heart to have this ceremony. I filled out the necessary papers today. They will certainly reach you tomorrow or the day after. Perhaps it might be preferable for you to send a little word to Pierrette to let her know the day when you plan to see her.

Now I warn you that the rejection of the pardon may be followed quite quickly by my execution. One never knows the time until an hour or two before it takes place. Only Baudet can let you know the date of his summons to the President's office. It will be good to act very quickly after that, at least, if you could come to Paris soon and celebrate the marriage a little before his summons. I don't know too much about what the ordinary administrative arrangements would be.

I have asked Pierrette to go to Confession and Communion. She will do this. She is waiting to have the faith to pray, and does not want to pray for this faith. It is a vicious circle which may last a long time. Patience! Things seem to be going just a little better. I believe she is beginning to understand that she has to drop all analysis of her feelings, and be concerned only about making an act of humility and faith in the dark, which will be quickly answered.

Little brother, I hope so much to see you here soon. I pray for you every day. Pray for me too. St. Therese of the Child Jesus said on her deathbed, "If people only knew what an agony it is, how they would pray! One should pray much for those in their agony."

Good-bye, little brother, I leave you and embrace you in Christ Jesus.

Jacques

It was a week before his death when he begged, with the
insistence of a dying man:

Do not worry too much any more about Veronica and the effects
of all this on her future. We must have confidence in God. What will
happen tomorrow, no one knows! We must give her the only good
which no one can take from her. God will help you in the measure of
your confidence in Him. But man is so constituted that he depends on
himself first, and only afterwards on God... I am at peace, I can't
manage to be even a little upset. It seems to me that what is going to
happen is the most natural thing in the world. You see the goodness of
God, who not only promises me an eternity of happiness, in spite of
all my sins, but carries me there in an armchair, with all the gentle
goodness of a father who loves his children!

On September 28, he writes:

No harm shall come to me, and I shall be carried straight to
paradise with all the gentleness bestowed upon a newborn child.

# CHAPTER 13

# JOURNEY'S END

Jacques knew that he had only a few more hours to live. Would it be tomorrow? The day after? The Lord was near…

Warned by his lawyer on September 24th,[1] he wrote his last letters, letters of farewell, letters full of unwavering faith and of hope which looked to God for everything.

Here is the letter to his prison chaplain:

Dear Father,

Here I am at the close of my life, my soul at peace and my heart steady. In a few hours a new and eternal dawn will break for me, if our Lord judges me worthy to be counted among His children. In these last moments I can hardly help reviewing all the scenes of my past life in the radiance of the new light that is mine as I stand on the threshold of life. They are not sad, because they have led up to the love of Jesus, thus taking on a meaning I never suspected. Some are even happy, and here I am thinking of those hours I spent at the foot of the improvised altar in a prison cell, or the time passed in reading the spiritual books your goodness knew how to choose for me — always the best!

I owe you my heartfelt thanks, Father, for your perseverance in my regard, for your kindness and the care you have always taken for my soul's welfare, nourishing it faithfully with its one need: our Lord

---

[1] See *In Five Hours I Shall See Jesus*, Jacques' Journal, September 24 and 25, 1957, pp. 284 and 287. Edited by Le Sarment, Fayard, 1989.

Jesus Christ. I am trying to thank you at least in part here below, but although I may seem presumptuous in saying this, I cannot hide from you the fact that it is from heaven, whence all blessings flow, that I should like to be able to thank you.

I shall carry your name to heaven with me, written in my heart, and when the Lord allows me to cast a glance down to earth, I shall gaze into a dark little cell where a priest is celebrating the greatest of all possible sacrifices, uniting himself each day to crucified Love, and then I shall ask Our Lord to cast a gracious glance on his faithful minister and fill him with blessings.

Peace be with you, my Father, and may the eternal light soon shine upon you also.

Until we meet in God,

Your humble and grateful sheep,

Jacques

Next comes the letter to his lawyer, Baudet:

Dear Master,

I cannot write this letter without emotion, thinking that when you read it, I shall be in heaven! If only I could describe all its marvels to you in advance, let you taste the sweetness of the love of Jesus! Alas, the veil still covers my eyes for a few more hours, and when it shall be removed, I shall no longer be able to share my joy with you, and you will have to continue your struggle alone in the exile and the bitter trials which are the lot of God's children.

First of all, a heartfelt thank-you for all you have done for me. This gratitude includes, of course, all the pains you have taken as a lawyer, your professional care. But above all it is offered to the man of God who, with rare zeal and constancy, never ceased to guide this wayward sheep and lead it back to the Father's fold. Your perseverance and faith have always amazed me. It was a fierce faith at times! I have to confess that the nickname I have given you is "God's panther."

In any case, you have given me God. There's no doubt that without you I could never have risen above my petty horizon. Without you, the torrent of prayers which have drawn me out of myself could never have flowed with such intensity. "Oh," you will say modestly, "I was only God's instrument." I know it. But may the one whom God was pleased to choose to glorify His Name become holy and worthy of the greatest esteem because of the wealth of divine love he has transmitted. We adore the Host, but we surround the chalice, become sacred through its use, with reverence.

Permit me to assure you that in heaven you will have a debtor who, according to whatever merits our Lord in His goodness will give him, promises to plead your cause in his turn, with all the love which God will bestow on him. In writing these words, I am thinking especially of the hour of your death, and if Jesus permits it, I myself will be at your side to the end, helping you with my prayers.

Dear Master, in these last moments I can form no other wish for you but that you may become more and more like Jesus crucified. May the peace which surpasses all understanding flood your soul, and may the Lord protect you up to that last morning, when a new dawn shall break for you, at last and forever.

Until we meet in God, I embrace you in Christ Jesus and Mary. Your brother in God,

Jacques

Here is the last letter he wrote to his closest confidante, his mother-in-law, Madame Polack. He is wonderfully detached, far more concerned about the suffering of this woman he loves than about his own.

Dear Mama,

We have written each other so often during these past six months that in this last letter I can only encourage you to persevere in the way in which you have just begun, for now you know how to do it. Try to open your eyes wide and to see, behind what looks like punishment, the manifestation of God's love. [...]

Be at peace about me. God has given me the great grace of drawing me to Himself, and when you read these lines I shall be looking upon our Lord Jesus Christ. I confess to you that I am a little fearful of your impulsive reactions, caused by your profound grief. Remain calm above all, do everything in moderation, and try to bury your sorrow in the love of Jesus, who only awaits your appeal to come and console you. Leave all justice, all vengeance, in God's hands. This is my express will. Christ came to save the world, not to condemn it. [...]

Don't forget that God is love! With these lines, I entrust my little girl to you. Protect her wisely with charity and moderation. Consider that Jesus loves her infinitely, and that all that you do for one of His little ones, you will be doing for Him... Be sure that from above I will protect and watch over her with all the love Jesus gives me. Abide, you too, in the love of Christ, and you will see God.

Now my life is finished. "Like a little spring flower which the divine Gardener plucks for His pleasure" [Jacques is quoting St. Therese of Lisieux], so my head will fall — glorious ignominy — with heaven for its prize! I am happy...

Good-bye, dear Mama, and may the Lord keep you and all yours. I embrace you in Christ and Mary.

Your son in God,
Jacques

Here is his last letter to Father Thomas:

Dearly loved little brother,

When you read this letter I shall be in heaven and I shall see Jesus. Before this, of course, the grain of wheat must be ground and the grape crushed, but what should I fear, since I possess Jesus? I wait in the night, and in peace, for the powers of darkness to be unleashed against me, to kill me... As a light breeze carries off a spring flower, so the divine Gardener will come to pluck my soul and bear it off to Paradise.

Be sure of this, little brother, it takes more than a few hours of struggle before one learns what love is! I have my eyes fixed on the crucifix, and never take them off the wounds of my Savior. I never get tired of repeating, "It is for you." I want to keep this image before me to the end, I who will be suffering so little. He suffered so much for me — He, for me — and in His goodness He takes away so many of my sufferings that there is very little left for me to endure.

Dearly loved little brother, I look forward to love, to being inundated with torrents of delight, and to singing the eternal praises of the glory of the Risen One... God is love!

Have no fear, little brother, I am taking your name to heaven, etched in my heart, and if in the blessed eternity Jesus allows me to speak with Him, I shall ask Him to bless you and yours and all those whom you care for with tender solicitude. Jesus, in His divine providence, gave you to me as an older brother to watch out for the weaker, younger one. Now, it is I who will be given to you so that you may receive from heaven all the gifts God has showered on me through your prayers, and much more, since I shall be at the source of all mercy!

Go in peace, little brother. May your road be straight and simple, and one day lead you to where you, too, will rejoin our one Love with the good thief on the cross, who heard that day, "Amen, I say to you, this day you will be with Me in Paradise."

Until we meet in God, I leave you, little brother. If you can, watch over my dear ones, and don't let them ever forget that my little girl belongs to the Blessed Virgin! May joy fill your heart and may our Lord Jesus Christ, Father of all blessings, bless and keep you. I embrace you in Christ Jesus and Mary.

Your brother in God,
Jacques

# CHAPTER 14

# THE LAST NIGHT ... EXECUTION

It was the night between September 30 and October 1, 1957, the sixtieth anniversary of the death of St. Therese of the Child Jesus.

At la Santé, in the cell from which he would leave directly for the scaffold, Jacques was with his God. In these last moments he was living the agony of the Garden of Olives, and interiorly he shed drops of blood, for even with God close, death is always death.

But Christ was there. He was with Jacques to the end. For one last time, Jacques received from Him an extraordinary grace: the certain knowledge that he would go straight to heaven. He wrote:

I am calmer than before, because Jesus has promised me that He will take me straight to heaven.

Two thousand years after the event, Jacques was once more the good thief on Calvary: "This day, you will be with Me in Paradise!" He wrote the last pages of his journal:

My Lord and my God, I am going to see You face to face. Happy those whom God honors with martyrdom! If only I could give my life like the martyrs, who died rather than deny their faith! As for me, I am guilty. . . May my blood, which will soon flow, be accepted by God as a holocaust. May each drop wipe out a mortal sin. Like Jesus, I implore heaven that no sin may be laid to anyone's charge because of me, but that every action, every thought, every word may serve to glorify my God. Jesus, I love you!

One must be pure like Christ in order to contemplate Him. Jesus wills to take me with Him to Paradise. Jesus can do all things in us... I believe that I shall go straight to heaven.

Jesus is very near to me. He draws me closer and closer to Himself, and I can only adore Him silently, longing to die of love.

I wish, like little St. Therese of the Child Jesus, to renew with each heartbeat this offering to become "a victim of His merciful love, until that day when, the shadows having passed away, I may repeat my love to Him in an eternal encounter."

The execution will take place tomorrow, at around four in the morning. May God's will be done in all things. I am sure that in His goodness Jesus will give me a Christian death, so that I can bear witness to Him to the very end. I must glorify His Holy Name, and I know that I shall glorify it... I must be steadfast, and so I think of the procession of all the beheaded who give luster to the Church. Shall I be weaker than they? God will preserve me from that!

Suddenly the thought comes: no matter what I do, Paradise is not for me! Satan is behind this. He wants to discourage me. I throw myself at Mary's feet and it is better...

Bitterness of all bitterness! I mustn't forget that whatever my feelings may be, I can always overcome them with my will. And then, God is faithful, I mustn't forget that.

I'm going to recite my rosary and the prayers for the dying, then I shall entrust my soul to God. After that, on my bed, I shall meditate on the agony of our Lord in the Garden of Olives. But, good Jesus, help me!

I have recited my prayers and I am filled with peace and strength! In His infinite love, Jesus has heard my prayer and granted it. Jesus, I love you!...

I am calmer than before, because Jesus has promised to take me straight to heaven...

In five hours, I shall see Jesus! How good He is, our Lord! He doesn't even wait until eternity to reward His chosen ones. He draws me ever so gently to Himself, giving me a peace which is not of this world…

Good Jesus, who suffered so much for me and who still carries all my sorrow! Happy the one who puts his trust in the Lord. He will never be disappointed. God is love!

Peace has gone now. It has given place to anguish! It is horrible! My heart is pounding madly in my breast. Holy Virgin, have pity on me! Yet, with a little more effort I believe I shall succeed in overcoming this anguish. But I'm suffering all the same!

I hear disturbing noises. God grant that I may sustain the blow. Holy Virgin, be with me! Farewell to all, and may the Lord bless you.

This is the last sentence in Jacques' journal.

I wait in the dark, and in peace. I await love! [Extract from the last letter to Brother Thomas]

Jacques watched and prayed all night. He was standing when they entered his cell. He embraced his lawyer, but did not say a word. His face was drenched with suffering.

After having received final absolution from the prison chaplain, he received Communion, together with his lawyer.

At 5:30, Jacques' head fell.

This was the man men judged, condemned, and executed. This was the one whom the Lord, I have no doubt, called to "enter into life."

# CELL 18

## Unedited Letters of Jacques Fesch

# PREFACE

The success of *Light Over the Scaffold* — more than 81,000 copies have been sold at the present printing and numerous translations published — has inspired the presentation of a further series of prison letters of Jacques Fesch. This is also a response to the requests of many readers of *Light Over the Scaffold*. The latter book, first appearing in 1972, recounts the story of the tragic crime, conversion, and rise to the heights of holiness of that unique young man, Jacques Fesch, who died on the scaffold on October 1, 1957.

The supplementary letters included in this volume are addressed to Jacques Fesch's mother-in-law, Madame Marinette Polack, who died in 1965.[1] This woman, endowed with an exceptional mother's heart, was destined to strengthen Jacques against the temptation to despair. After his condemnation the two corresponded almost daily.

The appearance of these new letters calls for some background from the preceding years. The earliest ones show us Jacques immediately after the tragedy and not yet in possession of the faith. All the letters to Madame Polack written in 1957 after his trial could not be published, for want of space. In the ones included here we have tried to show Jacques Fesch's day to day struggle, pursued as he was by grace and tormented at the same time by his natural impulses. Throughout this period he was in the unenviable position of a prisoner condemned to death, for whom the realization of his terrible fate rapidly became a certainty.

In this new collection of letters we come face to face with

---

[1] Jacques' mother died of cancer on June 7, 1956. At the time of the tragedy she had offered her life that her son might die well.

Jacques' natural feeling of rebellion. We see the unfolding of his days
in prison, the world's attitude to him, and his overriding concern for
his family. His long solitude, and his human reactions, become palpable.

*Light Over the Scaffold* traced Jacques' early story, portraying
the atheist who became a believer who became a friend of Christ, one
who met the challenges of his faith with the ultimate degree of hero-
ism.

This present volume depicts the face, the heart of this man who
struggled in faith, suffered the agonies of a highly personal combat
and finally won through to that inescapable "yes" which God asked of
him.

As Leon Bloy put it:

> One does not enter Paradise tomorrow, nor the day after
> tomorrow, nor in ten years. One enters today, when one is
> poor and crucified.

Ultimately, the God who sustains man on his way of the cross
also, at the last, wipes all his tears away.

*Chapter I*

# IN PRISON

Jacques Fesch had placed himself outside the pale of society. He had been in prison since February, 1954. He did not yet have faith. But thanks to his solitude, he had come to a reawakening. He wrote to his mother-in-law:

*Thursday, March 18, 1954*

Dear Mama,[1]

It was good of you to think of me and write. You'll never know what a comfort this is to me. I am very unhappy, and still haven't been able to understand how it all happened. It's as if some fatal force had been driving me on. Everything has turned out so badly, so strangely. Still, I'm not losing courage, miracles do happen sometimes. But it's hard! How much unhappiness I have caused!

As for the photos, you can send them to me in the mail. I think about Veronica day and night, and this is the hardest thing of all. Dear Mama, I leave you and embrace you with all my heart, you and all the family.

Jacques

---

[1] Whenever Jacques uses the expression "Mama," he is addressing his mother-in-law, not his own mother.

Jacques had seriously wounded one man, had killed a
policeman, and in his flight had also wounded several other
people. Although he was carrying a gun, he had not set out
with the intention of killing. He was no hardened criminal, but a juvenile delinquent. In the course of the tragedy
he fled in panic, thinking only of escaping his pursuers.
Alas, one of his bullets caused a death. Jacques would
always think of this as an accident, and would therefore be
convinced that his condemnation was unjust. Yet he was
aware that he might have to pay a very high price. He was
imprisoned at la Santé. Three years were to pass before his
condemnation to death.

On March 24 he wrote once more, always to the one
who was to become his closest confidante after his condemnation:

*Wednesday, March 24, 1954*

Dear Mama,
I just received your kind letter and the photos of Veronica. She
is really adorable in all three of them. I have placed them on my table
where I can see them always. The possibility of never seeing her
again makes me realize what I have lost. She is the most to be pitied,
it is she who will suffer the most.

I am enduring my sad fate with resignation, and the solitude is
doing me good. I thank you for your concern for me, but the regulations are very strict, and I am not allowed to receive much of anything. The limitations are extreme.

I read a great deal, and the chaplain's almost daily visits are
helping me immensely. I still haven't lost heart completely. Fate is so
capricious and unpredictable.

Dear Mama, I embrace you with all my heart.

Jacques

*Monday,[2] March 30, 1954*

Dear Mama,

I received your letter and the little photos. They are very nice, but not as good as the large ones, where Veronica is more natural.

I saw Pierrette today, and my father. The sad part was having to look at each other through double grilles. I could hardly make out their faces, and the time was so short. I'm beginning to realize a little of the horror of this situation. The future looks so dark.

I didn't really mean to delay so long in answering your letter, but there are days when all I can do is lie motionless in a corner and reflect. Everyone is very kind to me, which is a great consolation.

My little Mama, I embrace you with all my heart.

                                Jacques

Four months later, Jacques wrote:

*Friday, July 16, 1954*

2nd Division
Cell 88[3]

Dear Mama,

I just received your letter from B. and I hope you'll get this one before you return to Saint-Germain. I hope too that you'll have a little better weather in the days to come than at present; it hasn't been a very good summer. As for me, it doesn't matter much whether the weather is good or bad — I can hardly tell the difference in my cell.

I've been shut up here now for five months. In some ways it seems short, in others long, but either way it is wearing me down. All

---

[2] In 1954 March 30 was a Tuesday.

[3] After his condemnation he would be imprisoned in Cell 18, set aside for the condemned and having its own special regime and arrangements.

the same I am getting used to it. The hardest thing is to adapt. I always read a great deal; it's my only escape. Also, I'm working a little on my English. I don't know if it will be of any use in the future, but at least it keeps me occupied for the present.

Thank you for suggesting the postcards, but I can't receive them as it is not allowed. I see Pierrette about once every two weeks for half an hour. It's a short visit, but that is the usual time limit. I also saw Veronica once. She is growing, but she hardly recognized me through the double grille. Perhaps it's just as well.

Dear Mama, I hope your stay at B. will do you good. How I'd love to join you there. I think of all of you so often. I must close. A thousand kisses to all the family.

Jacques

*Tuesday August 24, 1954*

Dear Mama,

I received your two nice letters yesterday, and I'm so happy to have a little chat with you. My lawyer gets back from his vacation tomorrow and will probably come to see me on Saturday or Sunday. Of course I'll ask him to get the judge's permission for your visit.[4] I think you would receive it through him. He is a fine man, and influential. I think he understands the whole affair perfectly and is handling it on the level that suits him best. I have complete confidence in him. Also, he is extremely religious, perhaps a little too much so. If I understand him correctly, in his mind the idea of crime is the same as the idea of sin, and the idea of repentance is correlative with condemnation. Given the serious consequences of my crime, I sometimes wonder if he doesn't think privately that a heavy penalty would purify me more… For my part, I believe there are other ways of being purified!

Above all, he wants my moral conversion, and that certainly is

---

[4] Only three weeks before his execution, in September 1957, did Madame Polack obtain permission to visit Jacques.

the most important thing. In order to counteract my sluggishness and fatalism, he needles me on the subject of suffering. For example, I think we both believe in our hearts that my penalty will undoubtedly be capital punishment. I know well he doesn't intend to let a word of this escape him, nor do I! Just as well! It would be better to be hung at once than to live for months with such a threat hanging over one's head. Of course, this is obviously the best way of avoiding illusions about the verdict, but it is also the best way of becoming an old man before one's time!

The chaplain too is a fine person, like all good, simple people. There is something lightsome about his face, and his smile would soften a stone. He has had much experience with prisoners, understands their suffering and knows how to touch their souls while attending to their physical needs. So you see, I am well taken care of. All I have to do is entrust myself to them, and wait for the great day, which will probably provide me with a foretaste of the last judgment and the pains of hell.

To change the subject, I'm receiving long letters from Pierrette, who seems to be recovering her balance somewhat and who informs me that Veronica would like to take a walk in the sky! Poor little thing! Lolo also wrote me a nice letter from England. I believe she has taken a fancy to the open-topped busses and the royal guards — expensive taste!

And you, my poor Mama, I hope you are able to get a little rest and have not been worrying too much. Things look black, but perhaps one day the fog will lift and let us see a little patch of blue sky. I'm glad your holiday at B. has done you some good, but be careful, don't eat too many hot dogs. As for me, I'd devour a chicken from Wantzenau with pleasure! For the moment, I'm getting something more like dishwater.

I think very often, you know, of my little girl. I should so love to have her near me. But what can we do? Perhaps I needed this trial to open my eyes! But destiny has struck me a bit too forcefully.

My dear Mama, good-bye for now. I embrace you very tenderly.

Jacques

P.S. I forgot: when you write me, put 2nd division, Cell 88. Otherwise the letter gets lost.

Jacques remained a realist — he always would. The more tragic events became, the more he transcended them, and this saved him from despair or madness. He would not become an old man before his time. But he would be given the maturity of old age, and this would be his salvation.

*Tuesday, August 31, 1954*

My dear Mama,

Thank you very much for bringing me the chicken. I'll probably get it this week and will have a feast with it. It will be a wonderful change from the hard boiled eggs and sardines from the canteen.

I'm afraid the entrance door here must be very depressing. I only see the three or four doors which separate the cells from the vestibule when I return from instruction. They are all quite dismal looking, and leave me in no doubt as to where I am, but once inside my cell I get used to it, and don't think about it any more.

It's a good thing I am calm by nature. Some of the men here have attacks of extreme anguish. They feel stifled and want to get out at any cost, and this brings on nervous crises, with howling and wailing. I hate to hear it because I can imagine myself in their place. Fortunately there are others who show a remarkable stoicism, staying five or six years in one cell without complaint. Once I leave la Santé conditions will be better. I have at the most six more months. There's no use worrying too much. I have good reason to hope that things will work out well eventually. True, the horizon is dark at present, but this won't last forever.

I received a letter from Lolo in England; she will probably be ready to come home soon. I will answer her, but the letter won't go out before Friday, as I am not permitted any more stamps until then. Don't let her worry at not hearing from me.

As to what would give me pleasure, I thank you, but I can't receive much, only one package a month, and books.

I've done everything necessary to get your authorization [for parlor visits], and have written my lawyer a note. You should receive the permit soon, and then you can let me know when you can come to see me.

Dear Mama, my soup has come, and the mail. I leave you, and will write again very soon. I embrace you very tenderly. Kisses to everyone.

Jacques

*Saturday, September 4, 1954*

Dear Mama,

I received your letter and the chicken. The latter was excellent, but I have to admit that since I've been living on carrots and turnips my stomach can no longer sustain rich food. I feel a bit bogged down. Maybe I ate a little too much. It's nothing serious though, I'm really alright.

As to the difficulty between you and my mother, I know very well that things do not always run smoothly of their own accord. We often have trouble understanding each other. It can even be impossible at times. I am much afraid that this is the case. Clearly these stories of racism do not amount to much. But what can we do? I am keeping calm. It is just one more storm. The atmosphere has been charged for quite some time.

I received a letter from Pierrette, who must be at Saint-Germain now I suppose. She seemed rather sad. I wrote her by the same mail with my letter to Lolo.

The day before yesterday I saw Baudet. He is leaving this week to visit his mother who has just had surgery for cancer, and will be back by September 15. He will surely have your authorization by then. I don't know how your visits will be arranged, but in any case I don't think I'll remain in this region. There's a good chance that I should leave for Alsace. Thus I will be going back to the place I came from, but unfortunately not under the same conditions. But these are all guesses.

I hope your operation will not reveal anything serious, but of course it is never pleasant to be cut up. Dear Mama, I will stop as the mail is going to be picked up any minute now. Good-bye. I embrace you very tenderly.

Jacques

CHAPTER 2

# AFTER THE CONDEMNATION

The verdict was rendered on April 6, 1957. More than
three years had passed since the arrest. Jacques Fesch was
now a believer. But his struggle would continue until the
definitive triumph of the spirit.

We now take up the letters written after his condemnation. We shall follow him as he fights his way to victory. There are periods of hope, of dryness, of expecta-
tion, and finally of joy. Through them all, the man who
began as a criminal is transformed into one of God's chosen ones, the elect.

"I HAVE ONLY TO WAIT FOR WHATEVER COURSE
PROVIDENCE SHALL MARK OUT"

*April 10, 1957*

Dear Marinette [his mother-in-law],
I thank you with all my heart for all the love you have shown me
during the painful days I have lived through, and which will continue
for many months. I've gotten off to a very bad start, and I am wondering with some trepidation how it is going to end. Certainly we can still
hope, but with all the subversive activity being carried on against me,
we have to be prepared for anything.

I can't say I'm in especially good spirits, but after more than three years in a cell there isn't much that can upset me unduly. If it weren't for Pierrette and Veronica I think I could maintain a kind of inner peace, a combination of lassitude and resignation. I have the feeling that I am wrestling bare-handed with a mountain which is ready to crush me, and against which I am powerless. If it all ends in tragedy, Veronica will have had a strange father indeed, and her little soul will be marked forever.

The same holds for Pierrette. She has already suffered enough, and I believe she hasn't come to the end of it yet. For both their sakes, I should like to be able to go on struggling, but what can I do? ... As you must have heard, my lawyer was admirable all through the trial from beginning to end, and so devoted. He has been very much affected, and, sensitive and conscientious man that he is, I am quite sure he is reproaching himself interminably. He came to see me Sunday with a smiling face, but underneath he was very strained. He has already had one client condemned to death. It happened a long time ago, but that man's face haunts him still. If it happens a second time, he'll never get over it.

Now it's all over, and I have only to wait with resignation for whatever course Providence shall mark out. Thank you again for all your proofs of love, which help me to endure this trial. It is so good to feel accompanied and protected from afar, when all around me I feel only hatred and vengeance. I'm going to ask Baudet if it would be possible to get you a visiting permit, though I'm dubious since they are so strict about this. I'll let you know.

I'll write very soon. I embrace you with all my heart and all my strength.

Jacques

*Tuesday, April 16, 1957*

Dear Marinette,

I couldn't correspond with you yesterday at noon as I should have liked. I was to receive a visit from my lawyer, so I took a shower and shaved. Baudet brought me a report of public opinion which, it seems, is very divided. There are some fairly good articles on the affair itself, the way in which justice was rendered, etc. I believe things are not going too badly. Naturally, we cannot expect to have unanimity — that would be too much to hope for.

As for me personally, you see, everything was settled from the first day, and I knew it would be useless to try to go into this trial with an open heart and soul. Some interpreted my apparent coldness as courage, others as cynicism. I can assure you that it was above all my feeling of powerlessness in face of these higher destructive forces that made me stiffen and appear fatalistic. And in the end, nothing could have been better calculated to make me act like a robot than to hear the audience hissing, "He wasn't afraid to kill a policeman, and now he's trembling for his own carcass!"

I learned too that Pierrette was received on Sunday by Madame Auclair, the author of a biography of St. Teresa. I wasn't able to get an account of everything that happened, but I must confess that I'm always a little fearful about Pierrette's spontaneity on some occasions. Over-eagerness to explain everything often results in confusing the issue, especially for onlookers who are not able to form a true opinion about the matter on the instant. And yet she [Pierrette] is so brave, so tender. I shall see her tomorrow in the parlor; she is the only one who can get a permit for the time being. Baudet will work on the others after Easter.

For now, I have taken up once more my monotonous little life, alone and confined within these four walls. Of course I have a different cell and am under maximum security, with a guard at the door night and day to quell any possible rebellion or, more especially, any attempt at suicide. A light is kept on all night too, but fortunately it doesn't bother me. I am allowed to lie down as much as I want, I eat better than in the division and have a serving of meat each day which I take with a good appetite. For the rest, I can receive nothing except letters, whose number, coming and going, is unlimited.

I am actually a bit tired, and have no head for reading. I walk, I nibble, I sleep, I write. We are allowed an hour's walk each morning from ten to eleven, with our hands chained. In fact whenever we leave our cells we have to trail this hardware around. Fortunately it is just symbolic, but nonetheless not very pleasant. We're apt to end up with a watchdog complex.

Let's hope this whole business will come to an end as quickly as possible, and that people will forget about me. Do not be too upset on my account. I'm still in good spirits and hopeful. When the verdict was pronounced, it seemed to me that I saw and heard you, but I was so upset that I could see nothing clearly, and the police were in no mood to chat with me.

I also received Veronica's note. Poor little girl! She is so sweet. Some time ago I received a small photo of her, and I find her considerably changed. She isn't a baby any more, but a little girl with a lovely smile and long hair. I think the lower half of her face resembles Pierrette's and the upper half rather my side of the family, but perhaps I am mistaken? In any case, she writes very well and is making good progress.

Dear Mama, good-bye for now. I leave you and embrace you tenderly.

I wrote to Simone.

Till tomorrow,<br>Jacques

Saturday, April 20, 1957

Dear Mama,

Your stationery is fragrant; you combine the pleasure of eye and heart with that of the sense of smell. When I shall be able to see you, it will be for me a little ray of sunshine in the midst of the storm.

You shouldn't take everything Baudet says seriously. Sometimes there's a little gruffness in his manner which can be disturbing, but once you know him you won't take it to heart. As to the witnesses, I have left him free to plan his defense in whatever way he thinks best.

You see, nothing will do much good. When, a few days before the hearing, this sentence dictated by the police appeared: "If Fesch is not condemned to death, we will go on strike at the Queen's arrival,"[1] I could hardly hope for much. The prosecution has twisted the facts in order to gain its end, and the best testimony in the world would be of no use.

Pierrette writes me that she was bitterly disappointed by the rank trick a journalist played on her. This is typical of the present state of affairs. Do not be too disturbed. All is not lost yet, and in spite of all the hatred and vengeance there is still good reason to hope. I trust in Providence, which knows how to choose what is for the best.

What bothers me most is my own state of mind during recent months. I believe I have changed in many respects; I have the feeling I am much harder, more savage, than I ever was before. I do not have true humility, nor the ability to forgive, like Pierrette for example, and I wonder how I will end. What an odd son you have! But don't disown me, for all that. If the guillotine doesn't devour me, there may still be some bit of good to be found in me.

I received a telegram from my friend the monk (who lives in a little world of his own with his feet off the ground). He wrote me: "We'll soon meet in heaven," which is touching from one point of view but a little too precipitate from another. I'll have to answer him in more moderate and down-to-earth terms. Ah, these monks! [This is his Benedictine friend Brother Thomas — see *Light Over the Scaffold*.]

Now we'll have two gloomy days, Sunday and Monday, with the silence of the world beyond the grave. No mail, nothing to disturb the monotony of the interminable hours. But I must stop this. I feel as if I'm on the verge of whining, and there has been enough of that already.

I thought a great deal about you and Veronica yesterday, picturing you wandering around on donkeys. What kind of little girl is she? Cheerful and full of joy? Or withdrawn and sad? It's terrible not know-

---

[1] The Queen of England.

ing, and I'd so much like to hear all the questions she must be asking herself about me and about certain other things. I hope she'll remain a child as long as possible. The day she grows up, I fear there will be much suffering in store for her, and sensitive as she must be, she will suffer twice as much. Alas, what can we do? Misfortune is blind, and knocks most often at the doors of the innocent.

Dear Mama, I hope your Easter holidays weren't too bad, and that you aren't worrying too much. Here comes the soup, and the mailman to deliver and pick up mail. I've been on the lookout for them both. Until Tuesday, then, I embrace you with all my heart.

Your little boy,
Jacques

*Tuesday, April 24, 1957*

Dear Mama,

I hope you enjoyed the Easter feasts and took advantage of the good weather. As far as I can see, you are being drawn sensibly towards mysticism, and I was very much touched by your spirit of sacrifice. As for myself, I have been content for a long time with a half-hearted tepidity. It's not that my faith has failed, but that I am weary and exhausted with sending vain supplications up to heaven which seem pretty ineffectual from this world's point of view. It goes without saying that there is a clear plan behind all that happens, and a higher will directing human actions and subtleties. What appears to us to be absurd and unjust, because we see it from below in an unfinished form, surely takes on its true significance up there. All I can ask for is a spirit of submission, of acceptance, and even of offering, and this will not be refused, but it is useless to ask for anything else. It's very complex and somewhat beyond me.

I didn't have very pleasant holidays, since I was more bored than usual and didn't know what to do with myself. I have lots of books to study, but what's the use? So I browsed in a few of them, and wrote a bit.

Pierrette hasn't sent me anything, but I'm going to see her this afternoon at about three. I just broke this off for a few minutes to go for a walk. It isn't much of a distraction, but it changes the atmosphere a little, and I can have just a few words with my neighbor. This afternoon I'll take a little snooze after dinner, then I'll roll some cigarettes and write for a while. You must think I'm very empty-headed, and disturbingly indifferent. I'm aware of this, but can't do much about it. Something has happened to my sense of balance, and I often envy you your spontaneity and frankness and your very human reactions. It seems as if I were doomed to be always analyzing my thoughts and feelings, a kind of censuring process that constrains me to say and feel whatever seems suitable and appropriate. I'm a real Englishman, forever maintaining my composure so as to be the perfect gentleman. I suppose this must be terribly tiresome for others, who would probably like to shake me, to make me react spontaneously. But you know me, you know what you are dealing with.

I hope you're going to send me some photos, so I can see if you have changed. I can picture Veronica perfectly, pulling your sleeve to make you hurry and buy her some of those plastic animals. How I should love to see her and get to know her. I have no idea how she may turn out, what she will become. Oh well, these are vain regrets....

Good-bye. I embrace you with all my heart.

Jacques

*Thursday, May 23, 1957*

Dear Mama,

I wanted to write you at length this morning, but couldn't settle down to it. Yesterday I saw Pierrette with Papa, whom I hadn't expected. What a visit! I'm exhausted, almost ready to scream, and I'd like to send everyone packing for a while... I'm sorry I let myself be carried away like that. When I think of this old man, so stricken, so deserving of pity, not seeing very clearly and not even able to walk well by himself, I fear that he may have been a bit pained by my conduct toward him! Yet in spite of all this, he has developed such an unconscious pride and egoism that I instinctively recoil from him...

He must be so unhappy, and he tries so hard to conceal the fact. Eccentric by nature (and I have inherited a bit of this from him), a mixture of cynicism and rigidity, and at the same time of basic goodness and extreme sensitivity. How many fathers would not have abandoned their sons long ago? ...

You ask how I act with Baudet. I think I am rather reserved with him, and only show the surface, because, having similar characters, we often clash. On the one hand I like him very much, and admire him tremendously. But from another point of view, there is a kind of stiffness about him which keeps us both reserved with each other. Then too, I always get the impression that he is living a mystical dream, and trying to concretize this dream and project it onto others. All the same, I am very glad he comes to see me so often; there are few who do.

I must close, as they are collecting the mail. Big, big kisses. Until tomorrow,

Jacques

*Friday, May 24, 1957*

Dear Mama,

This is a good morning, more so than most. I feel better somehow, I'm not sure why. Anyhow, it's all to the good, provided it lasts.

I received your last letter yesterday. I'm enclosing three little drawings I made yesterday [Jacques sketched in pencil on the backs of his cigarette packs]. I can't cut them out, as I have nothing to do it with, but perhaps Veronica can learn the fables of La Fontaine from them. Tomorrow, if I can find a pin, I will send you a beautiful camel. I will make little holes all around the outline, and then I'll be able to detach the drawing.

Thank you for the little yellow chick. I put it with the thrush on the back of a colored postcard (Velasquez' *Christ*). The color combination is delightful. I can easily picture Veronica making that little chick. She must have worked very hard at it. If I were outside, she herself would offer me the little chick in person! Oh — it's time for our walk. I must go at once.

[Jacques interrupts his letters, then returns to them, without making any break in the writing. He never starts a new paragraph. This is in order to save space, as only a certain number of pages is permitted.]

There, that's over. Unfortunately it is raining, and I had to wear enormous boots, like a farmer, so as not to get my feet wet. I had breakfast, too — a little fish and a small glass of wine. It wasn't bad, but now I'll have to wait until tomorrow to eat again, though I'd be glad of something else in between! ...

Don't send me cartons of cigarettes; they would be taken, and anyhow I have some here.

How did you like my little women? I'm looking for ideas, and when I've found something I'll make a little drawing and send it to you. I used to make nice dogs, but I've forgotten how to do it, and as I'm not much of an artist...

Well, it's late and I hear the mailman coming, so I'll close this letter quickly and give it to the guard. Until tomorrow, then. Have a nice Sunday, and hug my little girl for me.

I embrace you with all my heart.

Jacques

# CHAPTER 3

# PURIFICATION

Jacques, in this letter as in many others, too easily attributes to God all the trials he is enduring. It is "the will of God," there is "a determined plan," and it all has no other object than "his purification" and ultimately "his good." Now it is not true to say that God wills suffering. What happens to Jacques is not the result of God's will but of the will of men. On the other hand, it is true to say that the love of God is always present and available to the one who suffers. And he may, if he opens himself to this love, transform what is negative into something positive. In other words it is man who, strengthened by God's love, can cause unfortunate events to become "providential" *for him.*

*Monday, May 27, 1957*

Dear Mama,

Today is Monday. It seems to be getting cool again, and I'm going to keep my windows closed so as not to catch cold. Yesterday it was very beautiful, and I was not too tired. Through the open window I saw lots of little balloons of all colors, with something hanging from them, flying up eagerly into the infinite freedom of the blue heavens. Lucky things! I thought of the film *The Red Balloon*, where the little boy floats through the sky with a host of friendly balloons. I must no longer have the soul of a little boy, for all the balloons flew off, insensible to my pleas. To console myself, I have drawn some pictures of frisky dogs. I'll send you one. It isn't a great success, but I can't be bothered to make another, so I'll send it to you as it is.

Last evening Baudet came to see me earlier than usual. Nothing much new. The "ticket inspector's" story was very annoying, and Baudet did not hide from me the fact that it could have very harmful consequences. Besides, a policeman was just killed a few days ago, but (fortunately) in a rather accidental way (after being kicked). This means, however, one more victim to duty, which doesn't improve the statistics and increases the general discontent.

I sometimes have the oddest presentiments! Imagination, perhaps? But I fear that a higher will, surely with some merciful purpose in view, is about to throw into the cogwheel of my destiny a destructive little grain of sand. I don't believe in good luck, nor in bad luck, but I am convinced that we are merely puppets with very limited freedom, making fruitless efforts to thwart the absolute. The only kind of freedom we have is inner freedom, but what do we do with it? We stifle it beneath our passions and allow it to be dominated by our flesh, until only nothingness remains, and our sensations resemble those of evolved primates. *Mektoub!* It's in the stars; it was willed by God. Don't think I am down in the dumps. I'm naturally laid back, but now there is a certain weariness and lack of interest in anything. I have no news from Pierrette.

I've just come back from a walk. I found a little bird, and caught it. How frightened it was! It acted like a little devil and I'm sure it's going to end with a heart attack one of these days. I wanted to bring it back to my cell, but then decided it would be happier outdoors, flying through the treetops, than closed up in this cage already occupied by such a strange bird. So, magnanimously, I opened my hand and it made off at top speed.

Good, here comes the soup. I'll be with you tomorrow. I embrace you with all my heart.

Jacques

*Wednesday, May 29, 1957*

Dear Mama,

A parlor visit today! I'm very glad, the day will pass more quickly. That's something over and above the pleasure of seeing a dear one, and not to be underrated.

This morning I got up earlier than usual, feeling less oppressed and a bit more self-assured. I think too that I have smoked a little less of late, which has helped to clear my head. To while away the time, I study a little, as usual. It doesn't seem like much, but by spending four or five hours a day with my nose in my books I'm painlessly becoming quite clever. But the more one studies, the more one needs to study. It's a hopelessly vicious circle. I made a modest effort to learn some mineralogy, and wanting to understand the intricacies of this science better, I have delved into atomic bombs and nuclear reactors. It is fascinating, but arduous and perhaps a bit useless as well, don't you think?

I just received your Monday letter. As you suggest, I will sign the little drawings, but at the moment I have no more of them. Forgive me, but I didn't know the 26th was Mother's Day. You know I have no calendar, and there's nothing to remind me of the important dates of the year. In fact last Thursday I read the Mass for the Ascension, and it isn't till next Thursday. I do hope you had a proper celebration, and I offer you my belated greetings and in my thoughts a great big bouquet of peonies (my favorites) with the compliments of Veronica (?) so prettily expressed.

Yes, I saw the article on the father of abstract art. I like his village very much, and the painting with the green background and yellow pylons. Unquestionably, there is a harmony of colors in his work which is impressive, and never leaves one unmoved. I don't really know how to draw or paint, but I should like very much to try to work out a combination of colors not found in nature, which might lead to unsuspected possibilities. There is a painter in this school who is dead now, but whom I used to love — Leger. I don't know if you are familiar with him, but his pictures are intriguing.

With the books in the library here I've found enough to read, and now I'm beginning to devour novels. At least four hundred and fifty since I've been here.

Well, it is getting late, and I must finish so as to get this letter off by noon. This afternoon I'm going to answer my monk, who has written me a splendid, very sensitive letter. It is really difficult to correspond with people like him, though. I feel like a raccoon trying to carry on a conversation with a dove in the clouds. I will do my best to be natural, but if he could ever see into the recesses of my soul![1] Good-bye until tomorrow, then. I embrace you with all my heart.

Jacques

P.S. I haven't written to Lolo yet, nor Simone...

Thursday, May 30, 1957

Dear Mama,

A sad feastday, long and dreary, fortunately almost over. I'm expecting my dinner any minute now, and if it comes, I shall have to leave you once more for a few moments. The trouble is, I have two little bottles of wine awaiting me, and after drinking that I'm apt to write nonsense. So if the end of my letter seems "odd" you'll know why.

I have spoken with Baudet about your visiting permit, but it's not an easy matter. Regulations for prisoners like me are very strict, and you have to ask a hundred times before you get one visit.

I just got my wine. It isn't very good, not even passable, quite near the bottom of the scale as wines go. But at least it is red, and has some alcohol content, so I mustn't grumble. I'm drinking it a little at

---

[1] Father Thomas, to whom Jacques wrote the letters in *Light Over the Scaffold*, the first part of this book and the first collection of his correspondence to be published.

a time… But forgive me, I'm talking about nothing but wine, and you'll be taking me for a drunkard.

Don't be too worried about me, in spite of the lassitude you may note in my letters. Brother Thomas wrote me a very beautiful letter, obviously a monk's letter, but it makes good sense even to a pagan like me. As to acceptance, and all the other things he requires, an offering of oneself would indeed be beautiful, but it is hard, and a bit superhuman. Who can do it? I don't feel particularly inclined to philanthropy these days, and obviously, what is written in theory is always sublime, but so far from what one can actually do.

You ask me how I felt on the evening of April 6 — [the day Jacques was condemned to death] — when I came back here. To tell you the truth I didn't feel very different from the way I have already felt for a long time. You, who are outside, cannot imagine the "milieu of justice." Some, many even, revelled in the theatrical atmosphere of the court sessions. As a journalist said, "There was no problem with judging Fesch; he had been condemned to death from the day he killed the policeman." What you feel more or less vaguely, I see clearly, and have for a long time. I know there is little that can be done because the opposition is too powerful. Besides, they have never concealed it from me: "Why did you kill that policeman? If it had only been a mere passerby!" As if the life of a policeman was worth more than that of any passerby! The most serious thing in all this, you see, and I would even say the criminal element, lies in the fact that the accused, who honestly tries to understand the opposite side, is unable to do so. Respect for the one being judged is absolutely indispensable. Contempt is out of the question, impossible. What does scorn achieve? And you see, it always comes to the same thing: it is impossible to hope, if one's hopes run counter to the materialistic and publicity-minded interests of some. This is why I always long to send "exhortations to patience and courage" packing… Well, I've let my ill humor pour out in a river of spiteful ink, just blackening the paper uselessly.

I'm enclosing a little dog and some birds. This dog is a bit more cheerful than his brother who went to you before. I've signed it. Until tomorrow, then. I embrace you with all my heart.

Jacques

CHAPTER 4

# ANGUISH, FEAR OF THE FATAL HOUR

*Monday evening, June 3, 1957*

Dear Mama,

I am in bed, so don't mind if my letter looks like a seismograph in the middle of an earthquake, with mistakes strewn through it like cockle in a wheat field. I have my nose turned toward the door and the window at my back, and feel a bit half-witted. I am watching this door, because I think it will open some morning upon a very odd spectacle. I am in the cell of the last man who was executed, and he, being in the identical position in which I am now, was greeted one fine day with, "Get up." And the rest... If anguish could materialize itself or leave its mark on the walls, what stories these walls could tell! But I am not superstitious, and not too impressionnable in regard to these stories (are there two n's in impressionable?).

Don't worry, I am not down in the dumps and I'm going to put an end to these reflections. And yet, the moment is coming, and will not be very reassuring, when I shall know that Baudet is with the President. The time will come for "perhaps the last parlor visit," and "maybe the last letter," and then I shall be lying awake for hours at a time, shaking at the least sound, and if ever a guard makes a slight noise as he passes my cell, I shall think they are coming to get me!... Well, let us wait. For the moment there is nothing to fear, and why should we trouble ourselves to moan before anything happens?

It is difficult to understand a prisoner because he suffers intensely from things that those outside would never dream of. You are not especially appreciative of being able to see clearly, yet if someone blinded you you would become frightfully unhappy, and all the stories of everyday life would be devoid of interest for you. It is like that with me. Being deprived of freedom, not being able to enjoy the fresh air, sunshine and the rest, makes a person far more miserable than you can believe. You see, the fact of dreading a fearful exit from here within a few months weighs down my spirit mightily, because I can imagine it all, and picture the scene in its full horror. However, I fear the final issue far less than the slow disintegration of body and soul in a setting where they can only wither.

That is why I wrote you that I did not care for the expression "courage." Not the kind of "courage" which you spoke of to me, but the "courage" of people who say to me: "Face the situation like a man, and take the consequences of your misdeeds, etc., etc." Idiots! I send them packing with mingled pleasure and fury. Baudet's arguments were somewhat like that in the beginning, but not any more! Well, I'm rambling on and I'm sure you must be bored stiff.

Till tomorrow, then. I embrace you with all my heart.

Jacques

P.S. I embrace you most particularly with all my thanks, for your very delicate gesture regarding the bracelet [given by his mother-in-law to his wife in his name]. I always feel that I'm so cold and indifferent in my letters, that people don't know what to make of me. Do you feel this way too?

*Wednesday, June 5, 1957*

Dear Mama,

This morning I got up at 6:30. I couldn't sleep any longer, and am wondering what's the matter. At 7:00 I had Mass in my cell as almost every Wednesday, then I had breakfast, did a few exercises, washed my cell and washed myself. I'm ready earlier than usual to begin my letters. As I write I am distracted by the spicy conversations of the prisoners who are taking their walk. Their language is very colorful, and if I could record the things they say, I could write a book which would portray a very authentic slice of life. What morals! In such surroundings, the best elements can't help deteriorating woefully.

But wait, there's the mailman! A welcome scratching sound at the lock, and behold... a letter. But I don't recognize the writing. It's a little card from my sister. She writes me that she couldn't obtain a permit. It is very difficult, and those in charge don't dispense them very freely. Patience. You know what that is. Form 8114 b, facsimile 51, corrected facsimile 55, to be filled out in 12 copies on special adhesive paper from Bengal, to be directed to the assistant of the captain in charge of the parlors in one's section. A favorable response to be given in eight months for... , etc.

This afternoon I shall see Pierrette for a brief half-hour. What a life it is, to be reduced to seeing her only through double grilles, and to be spied on and watched like an animal in the circus. What do you think happens when they suppress the freedom of a human being biologically designed to live freely? Look at history... Every oppressed person is like a volcano under pressure, and when the gases escape the effect is devastating!

Well, I shall stop rambling and eat. That will be more profitable than railing. Until tomorrow, then. Have patience in regard to the little drawings. Yesterday I did an ostrich, but I don't know where to place his beak, so I can't send it to you yet. I embrace you with all my heart.

Jacques

# CHAPTER 5

# JACQUES JUDGES HIMSELF

Jacques Fesch was far from having any illusions about himself. He knew what he had been. He knew what he had become. He knew what he could become, without special protection. He was sincere in denouncing the judgments that had been made regarding a situation unique to himself in all its effects, and which no other person could experience in his place. The sick man and the doctor both know the illness, but how differently they know it when one of the two does not experience it in his body!

*Saturday, June 8, 1957*

Dear Mama,

You are right when you say that "I am becoming a little wicked," especially when I feel like sending people packing. I see this very clearly in myself, and I often have the impression that I am extremely unfair. But you shouldn't pay too much attention to this, it is just the steam escaping, to prevent the machine from exploding. But this isn't to say that it isn't very odd for those around me. I can't keep peaceful; I long for a thousand things and these unsatisfied desires create a permanent state of revolt rumbling beneath the surface. This may help me not to fall into a state of deathly exhaustion, but there's a risk that it might land me in a very difficult position one of these days. Professor P. [a kindly correspondent] wrote to me: "Above all don't let yourself be caught in a prison mentality, which turns men into automatons and destroys all personality." He cited the example of a musician at Buchenwald, who prepared his future concerts for the day when he should leave there, and another who described for his friends the country scenes which he could observe from his window.

That's all very fine, but this little world which a man might create ends up by destroying the nervous resistance of the dreamer, and some day or other he must confront reality with its consequences: either revolt or exhaustion. Yet I believe there is a third solution, the only one which can bring peace and full enjoyment to the moral and spiritual faculties: faith. But who can have faith? Between a monk and a prisoner who is a believing, practicing Christian, there is only a difference in name. Can one ask persons who are more or less degenerate to raise themselves to summits accessible only to certain privileged souls? I don't think so, and I have yet to meet anyone who can prove that this philosophy could be effectively put into practice. So much so, that I don't yet see which is the better solution to adopt, if I wish to preserve all that differentiates me from an animal.

But I must drop this discussion, for I can guess that you are yawning with weariness.

No, your letters never "bore" me as you say. They always echo my own feelings, and are very comforting in their simplicity and frankness. Some people write from the heart, others simply to give pleasure. Both are acceptable, but I can sense the difference. I don't like the idea of those two days of vacation. I am going to be bored, and anything is better than that. I shall write, and keep my nose in my books. I'm beginning to become quite clever, and even if this has no practical purpose, it always keeps me occupied. The chaplain comes to see me at the foot of the bed. I am like an old, enfeebled bigot who receives the priest in bed. (I certainly don't mean the priest is in bed!). When I gave him my opinion about the "affair" and the judgment, he seemed to understand a great many things, and was quite moved. But you know me, I always act so reserved and stiff, like a well brought up young man, that people never know what to make of me. I'm much more relaxed when I write, and I was happy to be able to express my thoughts to him about the reality of the affair.

Before sending this letter, I'm going to try to write a little note to Pierrette, otherwise she won't get anything from me before her visit. Have a good Sunday and Monday. I leave you only with my pen, and embrace you with all my heart.

Jacques

*Tuesday, June 12, 1957*

Dear Mama,

This morning I rose at 6:30. I prepared my cell for the chaplain, assisted at Mass, had breakfast, washed my floor with a large pail of water, and at last, everything being ready, I am writing to you while awaiting the walk. As I told you yesterday, I received a letter from Strasbourg, very kind and very delicate. It is a friend of Lillian's whom we knew vaguely from our travels across the Vosges. I wonder how it is that some people have so much sensitivity and Christian charity. What difference does it make to them what happens to me? And how can she manage to feel such a compassionate interest in a stranger? I should be nothing but a stick of wood were I to remain always cold and insensible. At any rate, these are God's chosen ones. In the depths of their hearts they reflect divine love and are not afraid to give the best of themselves with Gospel liberality. As for me, I am a bit too degenerate to be capable of such heights. I must have inherited all the moral defects which have accumulated through generations of fast livers, and each time I try to lift up my head the weight of heredity is so powerful that it throws me back into my original and natural position, which is not a very happy one. I have gnashing teeth, and almost instinctively take refuge in stiffness and defiance instead of cultivating a generous spirit. Perhaps I shall end up in hell, one of those harmless little red devils. Not too bad — I might find myself among friends.

This afternoon I shall see Pierrette. It will be a pleasant half-hour, the midpoint of the week. Only, the more often we meet, the more we become like strangers, and when I shall no longer be here I fancy that in the end we shall forget each other altogether, which might be the best thing.

You ask me what the chaplain thought of the little paper I wrote for him. I really don't know for sure. He seemed to be much moved, and I was particularly glad that he was able to see the situation as it is, and not as he might have imagined it. I believe that this discovery of the truth has touched him deeply. People can be very odd, and imagine others to be either totally good or completely evil and inhuman, according to their own idea of good and evil. For some, at first I was a hard young man, cynical, brutal, sure of himself and cruel, fully aware of what he was doing and deliberately choosing a life of crime. And now, I am almost a saint! We allow our imaginations to soar, while we remain on the earth (literally and figuratively).

I am in the process of nibbling a chocolate and I think I've smeared it on the letter. Forgive me, I've become a little pig. Alright, I'm going to eat my soup. Yesterday I didn't take much, and today I'm making up for it somewhat. I dream of huge joints of meat, lobster with bowls of mayonnaise and mussels in cream!

I hope that things are not going too badly for you and that you are living in peace now that the painters and other annoyances have departed. I think of you a great deal, and embrace you with all my heart.

Jacques

*Thursday, June 13, 1957*

Dear Mama,

Yesterday I saw Pierrette, and yes, she gave me a hug for you (figuratively, alas) and also showed me the pretty little silver bracelet which shimmers like gold. She is pleased with it and plays with it as Veronica does with her rattle. So we both had our chains, similar in appearance, but I, being more spoiled, had two of them. I am writing in bed, which is not very convenient, and as soon as I let my head fall back on the cot I shall depart for the Land of Nod.

*Friday, the 14th.* I slept well and was awakened by the chaplain who came to say good morning. I kept blinking at him and muttering meaningless words which made him laugh. They are predicting a long hot day. I don't feel like doing anything, and I dislike being in this mood. When I am, the time seems so long. How I should love to be able to give you a hand with your garden. A hand with the spade, a hand with a Martini! Like the time when I was in charge of the mayonnaise. I wonder if your house is spic and span. Have you changed the color of the walls? I believe they used to be white. Has my sister had her hall and dining-room painted red? I can't quite picture how that would look. What kind of flowers have you planted? If I close my eyes I can see your house with its beautiful hewn stones and the strip of surrounding grounds. I suppose that is where you want to plant the flowers. I can almost see the peonies! But don't mind me, I'd have peonies everywhere. I love roses too, but only on trellises.

Have a good Sunday, and I'll write you tomorrow. I embrace you with all my heart, and have commissioned Pierrette to do it for me. Soon I'll send you another drawing, a little bird with a devilish air about him.

Jacques

CHAPTER 6

# HOPE... BOREDOM... FEAR... REBELLION

*Sunday, June 16, 1957*

Dear Mama,

Last evening I saw Baudet. He brought me some good news which you may already know. A few days ago the television program, "This Passing Life," presented a debate on capital punishment. Max-Pol Fouchet discussed it for a quarter of an hour. He considers capital punishment barbaric in every instance. He concluded by taking my case as an example, and according to Baudet you would have thought he was a lawyer pleading for his client, he put so much conviction into it. At the end he asked the TV audience to write personally to President Coty asking for my pardon! It seems to me that this was the best publicity I could have had. At nine o'clock in the evening thousands of people are watching TV, and this was almost an official viewpoint that was being presented. If only the President had been inspired to be watching at that time. The same evening, Baudet was invited to the home of a journalist who is close to the President in a professional capacity. That may not be too important in itself, but it is often little things that make an impression. A Swiss journalist also came to get information from him for an article. So at the moment the wind is favorable. May it blow still more strongly, and set my ship sailing toward freedom. Good night, until tomorrow.

Monday morning. I'm rubbing my eyes hard, trying to chase away the last vestiges of night. I slept badly. The storm woke me and I was stifling. Oh, for a bit of air! ...

I hope you had a good Sunday. What on earth am I going to do today? I've had enough of reading, and walking bores me. Well, I'll find something, even if it's only to write a letter or two. Only, it's too hot to think. I started a letter to the professor but didn't send it yet as I didn't know how to finish it... I've been for a walk, and feel a little better. Tomorrow I'll send you a little drawing of an animal. Before long you'll be able to set up a menagerie.

Yes, yes, I remember very well the time I stepped across Pierrette's balcony. Veronica was asleep in her little white bed, and each time I hugged her, I woke her up. I remember her saying, "Papa!" each time, and falling asleep immediately. Only, I didn't think she remembered it the next day, nor that she would be telling you about it now. You must be smiling! Oh yes! Everything could have been so simple. So much the worse, regrets are useless, what's done is done. I'd rather live with a positive outlook.

Well, Mama dear, good-bye until tomorrow. Don't wear yourself out with housework, and don't worry to no purpose. I embrace you with all my heart.

Jacques

*June 18, 1957*

[...]

Too often law and morality are confused! If I have acted badly, I know it, and above all I know how I have acted. I know very well that I wasn't free, and wouldn't have done what I did even had I been at the bottom of the social ladder. My real guilt does not lie there! It is not the actions which have brought me here that are especially serious. The actions for which I reproach myself are of a different order, and if one day I am judged in truth, it will be those which will be weighed in the balance. Pierrette, Veronica... For these I shall have to answer!

Obviously, the actions themselves have to be taken into consideration. Someone may say to me, "What about the death of a man, what about the orphan?" Should one judge on the basis of actions, or of intentions? In intention and in will, I am innocent of these criminal tragedies. Is the drunken driver who kills a passerby condemned to death? And as to the consequences? ... It is very upsetting when someone says to me, "You could have avoided acting in that way." I say no. I could have avoided leaving Pierrette, and it is this that makes me feel most guilty. To avoid the series of catastrophes which brought me here, I know was impossible. Let us call it fate, or the consequence of a defective education, combined with an innate weakness of character. I had all the makings of my own fall, and I have fallen, as might have been foreseen. But I do not appreciate it when strangers, who see the actions of others only from their own point of view, analyze and discuss the question. People don't care for mediocrity. They want monsters or saints; and feel let down by the affairs of insects. They are fair, more or less, and judge the acts of others as if they were in their place. Certainly, they would never have acted like that! Therefore, condemnation without appeal.

Do you know what I mean? When I see a man accused of infanticide I am horrified, because the idea is totally repugnant to me, but I do not condemn him, because I realize he did not see it the way I do. It's the same for me. I did not realize the gravity of my aggression at that moment, and people judge me as if I had been fully aware of my actions. There is only one justice, only one law. It tells us: "Do not judge, for it is not for you to judge men." And these words come from above!

One really has to be here to understand this. How is it that a prisoner condemned to death is unable to accept it? Quite simply because people are judging a man who did not exist, and whom they wish to consider as a free, balanced and conscious person, while the prisoner knows very well he was none of these things. Although he cannot even explain it to himself very well, he is wounded in his sense of justice.

You see, for people outside, my present case is something like this: "A criminal, brought to his senses by life in prison. His actions condemn him, but what he has become should save him." While the truth is this: "His actions are deserving of condemnation, but the man who committed them is perhaps less so. What he has become may perhaps be an interesting phenomenon, but he still cannot be trusted, for there is no proof that the evil which was in him will not surface again." This latter sentiment is more just, and closer to the truth.

Well, I'll stop now, and embrace you with all my heart.

Jacques

*Wednesday, June 19, 1957*

Dear Mama,

I have a pen that practically writes by itself. Forgive my diatribe of yesterday. I was bound to write you a weird letter. I was rushing to finish it before the mailman came, and I let the words fly at the speed of my imagination.

This afternoon I shall see Pierrette, a pleasant little half-hour which will lift me above my usual lethargy and make me regret all the more being here. After the visit I shall study a little and prepare my dinner, which will consist of fruit salad. Then I shall finish the day reading.

Physically I am feeling better. Morally, it's always the same, only my moods change. I don't get the impression that I am growing in wisdom and virtue, but quite the contrary. I seem to be reverting to the animal kingdom with rapid strides. That's the price one pays for being in prison. As the great Meng Tseu [Mencius] said, "Force and violence never produced anything but ruin and savagery." I like the Chinese philosophers very much. Their discourses, maxims, etc. resemble the phrases of the Gospel as two drops of water resemble each other.

You know, it is easy to say "accept," but far less easy to do it. A plant deprived of sunlight shrivels up and dies; a man in a cage turns bitter and naturally looks to his instincts for escape. I know well that there is nothing of the soft and tender about me. I am a creature of flesh and blood, inclined to live fitfully almost in spite of myself.

I understand well what you mean when you counsel me to accept my lot. Alas, I'm incapable of that, and moreover I've never found anyone else who could do it. That would perhaps be the only way to live in peace. But what is peace when you are twenty-seven? When spring and summer have passed, one may be happy to rest in the peace and tranquillity of an autumn lit by the last reflections of the dying sun. Then one lives on memories, while awaiting the death of winter and the great peace of the snow. But when it is spring, the blood races and the whole body is ready for combat and joy.

Mama, don't you see, no one can bypass nature's laws without paying the price? Whatever be his reason, the man who does not act according to his nature is heading for death, with a certain degree of control of course. I was just reading a book by the great pilot Rudel, a German who brought down hundreds of planes, and who endured almost every kind of suffering. He ends his book with these words, written as a prisoner: "Far better to die than live in a cage!" That must have been how the lion felt, when they found him dead in his cage with a twisted bar in his mouth. He had expired in a final paroxysm of rage. (Don't worry, my teeth are bad!)

I know very well what you are thinking, and I understand. One sees the best solution but still cannot deal with the problem positively and realistically...

There, I've gone on at great length about something not too important. Don't despair of your little boy all the same. If the little guillotine doesn't devour him, there may still be some hope for him. Until tomorrow. Have a good rest, and plant your geraniums with care. That will certainly be beautiful, a mass of red against the white wall of your house. I think of you often, and embrace you with all my heart.

Jacques

P.S. I too would love to be in a sail boat with you. And I think the sharks would like it also.

*Friday, June 21, 1957*

Dear Mama,

You won't get this letter before Monday. In a half-hour we have our walk. I will speak with my neighbor, a nice young man who is not, and never was, spoiled by fate. Our affairs took place at the same time, only a few days apart.

It used to be terrible before. Prisoners were all together in the same cell, and when they came for one, each imagined it would be himself. Baudet knew one of them who was awakened very early every morning and asked what his name was! He couldn't speak and developed a heart condition. It wasn't him they wanted, but his neighbor in the next bed! It was a severe blow.

You see, almost instinctively I come back to these stories about the sick. I'm going to get ready for my walk. I can hear them counting chains outside the door. It doesn't bother me too much any more. I have a very slender hand and when I twist it a little it's no broader than my wrist. The hand of an artist! I'll finish this letter after the soup. . .

Here's the mailman. I can recognize your handwriting from a distance, and I'm feeling the letter with my fingers to see if it's thick. It's crazy, but whenever I receive a letter my first reaction is always one of fear. I'm afraid to get bad news, and yet God knows there never is any. There is also a second letter, with handwriting I don't know. I open it... Two pages. One from Brother Thomas, the monk, and the other in pencil or diluted ink, from a young girl I don't know, who signs it, "Your sister Frances." Exciting! Yummy! I'll tell you what she says. Oh, Frances, that's a lovely name. Good, I'll read all these in peace. Until tomorrow and Monday. Have a good Sunday, and big kisses.

Jacques

*Sunday, June 23, 1957*

Dear Mama,

Yesterday I saw Baudet, and his news was rather interesting. My final appeal will take place on Tuesday at the same time as my neighbor's, that is, in all likelihood — since the lawyer for the appeal is going to try to have it postponed. The reason is that if our two appeals take place together, our two pardons would also be only a few days apart. To pardon one condemned man is acceptable; to pardon two is also acceptable but less certain. It would be better to keep the two as far apart as possible. There are not many reasons for an appeal. My neighbor doesn't have a real one, but it seems that I have a serious enough one which might lead to my returning for a second court trial, but we can't count too much on it. I shall know this week, and if the judgment should be reversed, you would see it in the papers, or at least in some paper!

The TV story has received considerable attention. Fouchet went to find Baudet with the letters he had received. Many asked for a pardon, but others on the contrary wrote expressly to protest the program and were clearly not benign in their conclusions. You would have to be filled with hatred through and through to take the trouble to write such things. The Elysée was evidently packed with letters. Gently but firmly they let the TV people know that it would be better not to be so virulent. The director asked Fouchet what he intended to discuss in his next program. "The same thing," he answered. At that point those in charge decided they would have to cancel it. Congratulations to this gentleman, who has the courage of his convictions and would rather lose the profit of a program than give up the fight he has undertaken. This is really beautiful and rare, and I wish I were able to thank him. Of course the police syndicate has covered over such a scandal! So you see the commotion, and my poor person has become the stakes in many battles taken up in other countries to some degree.

The letter I received from Frances yesterday was very touching, really sublime in its fine sentiments. She has two children whom she must bring up alone, and a husband in an insane asylum. She is filled with joy and peace, and her letter has a fragrance about it that is not of this world. A pure heart, a simple and generous soul who knows only how to give. I prefer not to make any comparison with myself, I'd come off so badly.

There is also a shopkeeper in Saint-Germain who has written Baudet a beautiful letter and sent me a little statue of the Sacred Heart. It is Madame B... . She is a very religious woman, who was much upset by the judgment. I would never have dreamed of the ardor and religious faith beneath her respectable bourgeois exterior. One discovers a hidden world beneath all these appearances, and in many a damaged vase, one can still find some fragrant flowers which restore one's courage.

And then, of course, I also received your last letter, in which you scold me furiously like a matador attacking a young bull. You are right to be frank and I understand very well. But... but... the sublime and I don't go together. First, you know, "the rising wind" can be so strong as to reduce me to a few inches in height. I don't want to pose as an interesting victim, but it really is a risk, not to be ignored. The chaplain is of this opinion, Baudet also, and a good many other people as well. The affair has had such publicity that the conclusion is bound to be the result of public opinion. No one knows what this will be, but too much optimism is as presumptuous as too much pessimism, and it is better to be ready for anything.

On the other hand, you see, I, being here, can easily see what prison life is like, what I may expect, and the consequences of inimical influences which I may have to face. When one does not actually participate in a trial, one views it intellectually, a little bit symbolically, and one is quick to draw wise and constructive conclusions whose only flaw is that they are a bit too sublime and do not take into account the factor of "flesh and blood." The mind is quick, it avoids earthly contingencies, outstrips time, and does a pirouette, all with the speed of light. The flesh is weak, it crawls along groaning, and cannot be hurried without danger. As for the sufferings of the flesh, no one can imagine them for another.

A man of faith who is dying of thirst will sell his soul for a drop of water. To judge him coldly (while one's own throat is soothed) is despicable. You know, you have to watch out for Epinal's pictures — they exist only in albums. You see, when Pierrette comes and bewails her life as seeming to hold no future, I try to comfort her. I see her living an upright life, with wisdom, and thinking only of her little girl's future, and I tend not to appreciate at their true value her feelings of abandonment, her solitude, and all the repressed desires struggling within her. Now, I understand better!

Do not think I'm writing these lines with a selfish purpose in mind. I'm like everybody else, neither wholly bad nor wholly good. I know I have a little girl and she's never out of my thoughts, but I fear there's nothing I can do for her. Mama, be sure of this: the day I leave here, it is I who will need her, rather than she me! You were at the trial. You saw how much importance the prosecution attached to an innocent child! Death for her father, and no pension for her. It will always be like that. The law is so constructed that I shall be more of a nuisance to it than anything else.

Mama, there will never be a pardon for me, never! For the last three years that I have been here, I have had proof of it. Do not imagine that people are eager to uplift anyone, or to rescue what might still be saved. Rather, look at the jury: "No, no, no!" A pitiless attitude is the norm, together with a most profound egoism in general. Look at the Seznec affair! and how many others. Don't imagine that one day they will open the door for me, saying, "It's all over now. Good luck, and a new beginning." They will never do that.

What I should like to make you understand is that when one is in here there are only two solutions: either you rebel or you think of yourself as a monk. Extreme situations are handled in extreme ways.

Well, I'm going to leave you, since I can't go beyond the sixty lines permitted. Till tomorrow, then, big, big kisses.

Jacques

*Wednesday, June 26, 1957*

Dear Mama,

I got up at 6:30 this morning. Incredible but true. I had to get my cell ready for the chaplain who came to say Mass here. So I had to be very good-humored this morning. At 7:00, I grumbled a little and felt a bit distraught. I didn't have the nerve to go back to bed and yet it would have been better if I had. I walked for an hour and suddenly felt very tired. I had no more physical resistance.

As to the appeal, I have no more news. Perhaps some will come today? At any rate I'm not counting on it in the least. The only thing that bothers me is that from now on I shall enter the category of those definitively condemned, and the regulations will be different. I'll tighten my belt at the canteen. Almost everything I receive will be taken away.

Last evening I was so bored I read the same book through twice. I was back in Florida with the bears and the dogs. I love animals and nature. I think I would have chosen this field for study. Geologist, naturalist, archaeologist, paleontologist. I have a precise mind which excels in classifying, sub-classifying, and retaining the most peculiar names, and then, it is all alive and real. I am not made for living in society; I get bored with it and wither up. I can't manage taking seriously what most people hold in high esteem. It all seems artificial and useless to me, especially man-made things.

On the other hand, to take an interest in stones, animals or plants is to set up a direct contact with the concrete manifestation of the divine laws. Sometimes I discuss this with Baudet, and ask him why it is that he has wasted so much time cramming his head with articles of law and obsolete decrees. He makes a face at me and doesn't seem to appreciate my point of view. But am I not right? Civilization has destroyed everything. What kind of a life do the men of our times have? Work on an assembly line, in a factory, in a subway station or elsewhere. When the most wretched of the Gauls at least lived in magnificent surroundings, and could enjoy simple, vital pleasures. Long live our ancestors, the Gauls!

Well, I'm going to take a walk right now. I have eaten, but it wasn't a very tasty meal. What I would have liked was a good dish of macaroni with plenty of sustenance for the "inner man." But when shall I ever savor this again?

This afternoon I absolutely must answer that young girl from Strasbourg. But it's so hard! If I am frank I offend people, and if I try to conform to what they expect of me it gets on my nerves and doesn't make sense. It's very difficult. If I never write you anything that shocks you, so much the worse. Get angry if you want to, but I shall say exactly what I think to you, without, of course, pretending that what I write is in complete harmony with the Gospel. What else would you want — it's such fun to moan and groan! Well, until tomorrow then. I embrace you with all my heart.

Jacques

*Thursday, June 27, 1957*

Dear Mama,

I feel better this morning, I've chased away last night's moths with a few brisk gestures, and I have a free hour before my walk.

Yesterday I saw Pierrette and Papa. The visit went well, and I didn't leave the parlor exhausted. It's only the grilles that upset me, you can't see through them very well, and then the bars give you the feeling of being a dangerous animal. Well, it's the rule.

Yesterday at noon I received your nice letter, which is very touching. Of course I believe in your tender affection for me. I have never doubted it for an instant. But you know, you don't need to be excessive with me. Nothing is really too important, except for certain things which do not depend on man. In all that has happened, there is a will which is manifest, and surely with a constructive end in view. I believe that at the last, some good will come of it all, and that nothing is in vain. Only, we shouldn't count too much on earthly help, or even on "reversals of fate."

To do well, one should accept everything that happens and keep one's balance despite the contingencies of this world. Only it is very difficult; one needs an iron will, and one often falls flat on one's face. But even from a fall one can learn something, if only humility, and the futility of one's efforts. One could say that the Lord plays cat and mouse with us. In some cases He allows us to proceed effortlessly, with a smile; then with brutal swiftness success disappears down the drain, no longer to be found anywhere!

The only indestructible things which last are the memory of what one has had, and the certitude of what is. And in truth, life is most beautiful this way. We swing from heights to depths, from rebellion to submission, and at each moment there is the possibility of total forgiveness. The only real unhappiness is to remain indifferent and tepid, as I used to be.

Everything is grace, they say, and I believe it. This applies above all to the things that appear to men as catastrophes. Each one is enlightened in the way that suits him best, and this light should serve to show him his destined path. One has far more forebodings than one can understand. It is all very complicated. There are almost as many kinds of religions as there are people.

You know, I love the chaplain very much because he has had a lot of experience with people, and especially with those who are suffering. He understands better than anyone what one may expect of others. He is kind and sensitive, and I've never seen him wound anyone by his intransigeance. He always seems pained by what happens, and understands perfectly that everyone cannot be like the Curé of Ars! And where would infinite love pour itself out, if the greatest forgiveness were not extended to the greatest misery? This, I suppose, is what eternal happiness consists in: to see clearly one's own absolute failure, and to know and enjoy the splendor of God.

You see, I am often annoyed and wearied when people say that the change which has been effected in me has taken place on the purely human level. I know better than anyone what it is. From the point of view of many, I could have avoided what happened. They believe I acted badly because I was a fully conscious and rational criminal. That was one part of my life. Now, they think, I have seen things clearly, I regret my action, and being transformed I want to repair the evil I have done. That, presumably, is the second part of my life. This whole idea is false! My life is one complete whole.

The roots go much further and deeper. We consent to the evil of the years, and nothing happens! Without being aware of our diminishing freedom, our body grows feeble and our will atrophies. Generations continue, ever transmitting a little more of their decay, until the day when the evil becomes so much a part of the individual that he can no longer act freely and is caught up and swept along in the destructive current.

It is at this point that a man discovers grace! Read the Bible, the history of men and races! It is always the same thing. Time falls away; there is a fundamental solidarity between us all.

Very well, I stopped there and had breakfast. I ate well, being very hungry. I would prefer to keep down to earth for the moment — it will help my digestion!

I think you will receive this letter tomorrow, and the one I write tomorrow, the day after, before Sunday. Dear Mama, I leave you, and embrace you with all my heart. Until tomorrow,

Jacques

*Saturday, June 29, 1957*

Dear Mama,

How hot it is today! I am staying in my cell in my undershirt; the thick walls make it relatively cool. I'm still sleepy. I think that I stayed in the sun too long yesterday; I'm not used to it and should be careful. After ten minutes my head was spinning and I had a pain in my heart. Now I'm being more careful, and will not expose my legs and hands.

I received the petals from my rose. They smell very sweet. The color is a bit faded, but I know so well what it should look like. Alas, you chose a very fragile symbol. Scarcely is it opened when it vanishes, leaving behind nothing but a beheaded stem garnished with thorns. I don't feel the least solidarity with this flower, and don't wish to have anything in common with it.

You know, "later on" as you say in your letter, I shall have considerable difficulty coming to give you big kisses. It is you who ought to come to see me. That's how things should go, with a little optimism. A man condemned to death has no rights, and never will have. It is a legal death! Once a pardon is given, it is given in perpetuity and then, according to the case and the prisoner's conduct, for as many as twenty years. But twenty years without counting his previous imprisonment! Consider my case. I have done four years, and now suppose I find myself pardoned "in perpetuity." After five years, the term is reduced to twenty, so I still have twenty years to do. A penalty of eight years would leave me fifteen, and including the time done, I would then have seven years to do. Four years later, they might grant me conditional release. I have done twelve years, and I would have to remain for three years on parole. That means someone would have to employ me and answer for me. At the least, I would be reintegrated for three years. At the end of this period, I would be definitively liberated. Only, for twenty years more I would be forbidden to travel. I would have to remain in one fixed place, outside of the large cities and principal departments [administrative districts in France], could do nothing independently, and could possess nothing. Every two weeks I would have to report to the commissariat to attest that I was still there! If any crimes were committed in my region I would be summoned to see if I were the guilty party. If I should unfortunately set foot in Paris or any other city, I would be imprisoned. Ten years later, I could take steps to have this interdict suppressed. So it would mean a whole twenty-five years always living under the cloud of civil death!

You see, Mama, there's no use entertaining any delusions. One never gets out of this situation. The only hope would be a foreign country. But of course, one would have to go abroad without permission. That would be very risky and one might run into many inconveniences.

I'm going to tell you a little true story. It is about someone I knew here. He is now fifty-five. At the age of twenty he was condemned to death, pardoned, and sent to Guiana. He remained there twenty-five years. When they suppressed the penal colony, he was pardoned. He was then forty-five. His entire fortune consisted of 135 francs! A few weeks after his liberation, being unaccustomed to the ways of modern life, he was run over by a car and became lame. Each time he returned to Paris to see the only parent left him, he was put in prison. A few months ago, he committed murder! Whose fault do you think it was? A celebrated judge once declared, "When you condemn a man to a year of imprisonment, you are condemning him in perpetuity." He should have known what he was returning to, I suppose. Have you read Carco's books?

Well, I will leave you for now. Have a good Sunday and you'll hear from me Monday. I kiss you warmly. Hug my little girl for me.

Jacques

*Wednesday, July 3, 1957*

Dear Mama,

It's too hot again today, and I'm in a daze. I sleep and mope about and haven't the ambition to do anything. So I'm inclined to be in a bad mood. From your letters, I see that things are not going much better for you. Let's rise above the storm and the annoyances. When it's a little cooler we'll be in better spirits.

If I wrote to you of the most I could expect, it was not in order to complain, but so that you could understand better what my frame of mind is, and that it is useless to try to plan ahead about more or less vain projects which will never be realized.

I believe Pierrette has come to understand this. She will have to organize her life without including idle dreams. Materially, I will do everything I can to help her. Even before, I was never able to make her even a little happy. It was impossible because I was too unhappy and unbalanced myself. But all this is past!

I am absolutely convinced that I was never free, and that everything that happened was willed and foreseen with a constructive final end in view. We are born with a hereditary potential. Can we free ourselves from it? I think I know myself well enough, and that is what worries me. I see myself going downhill from one disaster to the next rather than scaling spiritual heights. It is somewhat painful, because if Providence sees me as I think I see myself, it may very well decide, out of pure love, to prevent me from being lost by removing the occasion definitively. This would seem a cruel injustice were it not perhaps rather a form of great clemency.

So you see, I am envisaging all the possibilities, and whatever happens, I shall not rebel against what I can understand.

I sent a parrot to Veronica, and I'm preparing a little cat for her. You will have a fine collection of pictures before you're through. I leave you now. Until tomorrow, and big kisses.

Jacques

*Saturday, July 6, 1957*

Dear Mama,

My head is swimming, and my pen feels as if it weighed two pounds. It is very uncomfortable. I tried to finish the little drawing last night, but felt so flustered that I spoiled it. Then too, my pen works for a while, stops for a line or two, then goes again by fits and starts. So you see I have lots of problems.

Yes, I know that Veronica left with her friend Christiane and that she was very happy to go. Tomorrow is her birthday: six years old, this little baby!

If I am pardoned, it will be in October. I will still have four months to wait here, leaving in February, 1958, to spend two months at Fresnes, then to depart again, for an unknown destination. Once I get there, I'll have six more months in a cell, up to September, 1958. That makes almost five years in a cell! Did you ever see old solitary animals in the zoo, huge wild boars which cannot be touched by the fingertips without leaping up and growling? Well, I'll probably become famous as one of these. I am following a normal evolution, and as I have a withdrawn nature and love to see into the depths of things, the effect will be all the more striking. Above all, you see, I should want not to be judged hastily, and not to have someone else choose for me a type of life that would be wholly unsuitable, and that others only live in the realm of imagination. This is something of what I tried to convey to the professor who viewed the situation from an unrealistic angle.

Well, here's the soup. I'm going to fix a green salad with some tomatoes; that will be refreshing. Have a good Sunday. Until Monday, I embrace you with all my heart.

Jacques

*Wednesday, July 10, 1957*

Dear Mama,

With the cool weather my spirits are reviving. I feel better disposed and less gloomy. I hope that you too are feeling better. Yesterday at noon I received your last letter. Beneath the words I sensed the storm rumbling in the background. Do not worry so much, nothing is very important. Yesterday I also received a card from Pierrette who must have had a little trip around Dijon.

This morning I saw the chaplain, who seemed a bit more optimistic. In contrast, Baudet grows less and less assured. Obviously, he is encountering reserve everywhere, which is not very encouraging. I finally managed to lift his spirits. There is a little obstacle which risks putting us in a very delicate position. My neighbor is not going to present his request for pardon until the end of September, and mine would be granted in October, just a few days after his. It is too close. Besides this, at the beginning or end of September a very serious case, exactly like mine, is going to be judged. The man stands a very good chance of ending up here, and if I am still here too there will be three of us, two being held for the same reason. Which is to say that one of the two is going to spend a very bad quarter of an hour. This is what must be avoided. I'm going to speak to Baudet about it so that he can do what is needed.

This afternoon I shall see Pierrette in the parlor.

I spent last evening reading a little book on the mountains, illustrated with splendid photos. There are some Alpinists hanging onto the rock wall in such a way you'd think they had taken lessons from a fly! I should dearly love to engage in this sport, but unfortunately I get terrific vertigo. It seems, moreover, that fear is the cause of this. I wonder to what point my fear is responsible for all that has happened to me. I don't have enough faith, and this causes an imbalance. Perhaps a simple medication (insulin?) might restore my confidence in myself and in life. I can picture Baudet pleading this thesis! What a key to human life and happiness!

I'm going to eat now. I'll write at greater length tomorrow. I embrace you with all my heart.

Jacques

*Thursday, July 11, 1957*

Dear Mama,

Yesterday I received your two kind letters. Tell me quickly, what did the fortune teller say to you? Will my star begin to shine a little? It's more than time for it to do so. When I was very small someone told Mama that I would become famous, but with a dubious celebrity that we'd be better off without, and that a few years after that

I would leave for the colonies, where I would make any number of blunders; that I should then fall ill, and would end my life fairly young, killed by a knife! So you see, nothing is lost yet.

I am enclosing the first illustration of my little story. There are five in all. Each day I'll send you one of them, which will keep you in suspense, and you will be wondering how the story will end. The white rabbit still has one paw that is a little bizarre. It's not too important, but I have to fix it.

Yesterday I saw Pierrette. I only half expected her, as you had written me that she wouldn't be coming. But the day before she had sent me the little card from Dijon, saying we'd meet on Wednesday. Well, she came... She told me things are not going very well at work and that it is quite likely she will give up her job. I wrote her a note last evening, trying to calm her, but without much hope of success! I no longer have any influence with her; I can only gesticulate in vain behind my bars... Always problems! I hope your health is better, and that with this cooler weather you feel more at peace.

Well, I'm going for a stroll. It's sunny today, but not too hot. When I stretch out to get a tan I am horrified at the sight of my arms and legs. They are as thin as match sticks and white as an aspirin tablet. Only my hands get slightly tanned, but so little! Oh, for the day when I shall have strong arms! Well, to console myself I think of the seven million men who have died in concentration camps, many of them really innocent. You can't help thinking that life is really not very important, and that its purpose is to prepare us for death. Then why this contradiction of having flesh and nerves that cause us pain and that crave what is bad for the soul? Perhaps the conflict is necessary, but what a world!

Dear Mama, good-bye until tomorrow when I'll send the second episode of *The Young Girl and the Flower*. I embrace you with all my heart.

Jacques

*Saturday, July 13, 1957*

Dear Mama,

Last evening I saw Baudet's collaborator. The presentation of the appeal is over and it was refused, as I had written you. There are however a few interesting little details. The lawyer for the appeal pleaded at great length and brought forward several points which, without being illegalities technically speaking, are important enough to unsettle some minds. He spoke at considerable length on the influence of publicity on judgment, the manipulation of the police which had been planned ahead of time, the relations between the court and civil parties, such as the fact of the President's having dined with Floriot on the evening before the verdict was given, and the unanswerable questions which were put to the jury. The Court of Appeals deliberated for nearly two hours, and gave a negative verdict only with reluctance. However, since they could only base themselves on points of law, it was difficult for them to act otherwise.

This hearing will be useful just the same, since all that was put forward in the presentation petitioning for pardon will have to be taken into account. Then too, the secretary of the President of the Republic was present at the hearing and seemed favorably impressed. I am expecting Baudet this afternoon, and he will give me more details.

I am sending you the third picture in my little story. See if the little chick isn't nice! You will be wondering about her reaction, of course, but now the story is getting involved; it really should stop there. What is going to happen? You will receive the fourth picture on Tuesday and you will know. Until then, patience!

I went for a little walk, then breakfasted, very poorly, and received your letter of Friday. I was also expecting a letter from Pierrette, but it seems she doesn't care to write. Being at home once more with the family, you may not have much peace. It is true that the little ones I knew have had time to grow, and you must now be surrounded by nothing but young gentlemen who will soon be showing their need for independence by climbing out onto the balconies and sliding down the drain pipes. Do you know what I used to do so that no one would know I was roaming around? Well, I used to lock the door of my room and put a big sack in my bed, with a feather duster for a head… and look where I am now! *Fiat!* let destiny be fulfilled! After all, error and evil also reflect life. Don't orchids grow out of dung heaps?

Well, I'll finish this letter quickly. I hear the door opening. Have a good Sunday and Monday. Perhaps you will have your permit for Wednesday? I'm a little doubtful, they are so strict! We'll meet again soon, though. Big, big kisses.

Your Zou

*Wednesday, July 17, 1957*

Dear Mama,

I wrote you a letter yesterday, but what is the use of sending it? I don't know when it will go. Perhaps tomorrow, or perhaps in another week. The strike is bound to come to an end; it seems to be almost over. Yesterday morning the rebellion was at its height, and when I say at its height I'm not speaking figuratively. The fireman had to come and hose down several fires and the smell of burnt varnish pervades the whole prison. I don't think too much damage was done but there was plenty of noise. The prisoners, of course, were locked in their cells, with nothing to eat. Stirred up as they were already, this did not improve matters. No more walks, no mail, no visits of any kind, and mess considerably reduced. Everyone is grumbling and the anti-riot police who are replacing the regular guards seem somewhat overwhelmed. I don't believe it will last long, because this morning I heard some men being thrown down into the dungeon, not without some injury. Might is always right, and it doesn't pay to hurl yourself against guns. It is better, more profitable, to yield, especially when you are out-matched. Well, I hope that by tomorrow it will all be over, and that we'll hear no more about it.

Baudet came to see me Monday evening, but there's nothing new. He showed me the letters of petition he had received. There were many signatures of very interesting persons. In contrast, there was one from a "villain" who wrote, crossing out the text of the petition and replacing it with a preferred text of his own which the advocate general himself would not have disowned! People are strange! That he might think it, that's his opinion, but a person would have to be fiercely belligerent to go to so much trouble to write it out. Well, his sheet of paper will probably go to join another kind of paper which is ephemeral and, as they say, hygienic.

No parlor visiting this afternoon, and I doubt if I would have had a visit in any case, as I believe Pierrette has left. So much the worse; it will be next Wednesday.

You see, in all that is happening these days there are things which are interesting and instructive to note: peoples' depths, their viewpoints and mentality. I am a rather curious creature, and they turn their microscopes on me as one does with a slightly unusual animal in the zoo. I can hear their reflections about me clearly. They are not very encouraging, and are typical of the opinion of a certain category of individuals. If my fate should ever be in their hands, I should have few illusions; it is always useful to know where you stand.

*Thursday, the 18th.* Third day of the strike! I really thought it would end this morning, but it's getting very serious. Always police, not guards. I think the fire the day before yesterday did considerable damage. They are talking about the library through which it passed. If that is true, that would be a fine thing! No more books! In any case, still no mail, no canteen. My cupboard is empty and I am ravenous. Fortunately I have laid in a little supply of tobacco, so I'll be able to hold out for a few more days. By then I hope order will have been restored.

*Friday, the 19th.* Still the strike. It is really in full swing. Since today is Friday, it can only be settled Monday at the earliest. Great sport! No more kind letters to brighten my solitude. I'm beginning to get weak again since I haven't had much to eat. I hope you know about the strike, and are not wondering what happened to me. This is really complete isolation, and I — who already found the time long — feel as if the days are not moving on at all. What a life!

*Saturday, the 20th.* Still the strike. It will last indefinitely, they tell us.

*Sunday, the 21st.* At whatever cost, may this devilish strike be terminated. I ate my last piece of sugar at noon and have absolutely nothing left now. Perhaps tomorrow? One never knows, but I don't count on it. At noon I received a letter dated the 16th, written by the professor at the Palaiseau. A very nice letter, and very understanding. I shall answer it as soon as possible. He is really a fine man. This afternoon I will take advantage of the spare time to answer Brother Thomas, who must be wondering what has happened to me, then that lovely young girl of Vesinet, and Simon. I have a lot to do, but I don't much like writing when I have to be careful and pay attention to what I am saying. With you, at least, I am at ease. If I write idiotic things, I know you won't be put off by them.

Well, I'll finish this letter without enclosing the next drawing since it would add to the weight and the letter might not reach you. I'll enclose it in my next. Until tomorrow, when I hope to be free to write letters once more. Big, big kisses to you and all.

Jacques

# CHAPTER 7

# MANEUVERS OF THE POLICE UNION

*Friday, July 26, 1957*

Dear Mama,

I was awakened by your letter this morning, which was given to me very early. Don't be too anxious about me. Everything will turn out as Providence has decreed, and certainly with a merciful end in view. Whatever happens should be viewed with reverence. And submission and humility are the only appropriate responses when destiny deigns to take an active hand in our affairs. Moreover I firmly believe that it is quite occupied with me presently, with a disquieting zeal in no way designed to prosper my earthly life.

At noon I received a letter from Baudet which was very depressing. Pierrette must have told you about it, I suppose? In any case, this is what he said: "The day after my visit your dossier came before the High Judicial Council. They did not hide from me the fact that a decision might be taken on July 30! This unusual haste alarmed me. I immediately sent a memorandum relative to your pardon, and followed all the necessary procedures. I learned only yesterday that these had succeeded, despite the pressure exerted by the police union, and that your case would not be examined until the end of September. I assure you this has relieved me of a great burden… The delay which the President has granted will not affect the future decision, but it shows the seriousness with which, resisting all inimical suggestions, the head of the State will consider your fate…"

So you see, the enemy is active, and will let no opportunity pass without seizing it. The most serious thing is that during the initiatives

Baudet took, even though he encountered much human understanding, reasons of popular interest were often raised in opposition to him, oversimplifying the problem and casting it, as it were, within the framework of "reasons of State."

To sum up, I have had a nasty fright. And to think that during these last days, I never suspected all that was going on unknown to me! Had the response [to postponing the case until the end of September] been unfavorable, I would never in the world have been prepared for this kind of reversal! The family must have heard the news, and they must all be more or less upset too.

Courageous Brother Thomas, the dispenser of prayers and charity, has been informed about this by Baudet and has decided to come to Paris soon... Brave soul!

For my part, I am ordinarily quite phlegmatic, but now the least thing can set my nerves on edge. The policemen who are guarding us aren't very familiar with our regulations, and this causes friction. This afternoon, after getting a shave, I wanted to cut my nails. It was impossible to make the man in charge understand that I really couldn't do it while handcuffed! But the regulations prescribe that a man condemned to death must be handcuffed while he is being shaved. We had therefore reached an insoluble problem! ... I would prefer not to talk about human idiocy, but it really can become an insuperable obstacle. All of which is very upsetting.

Well, according to the latest news it looks as if the strike will end tomorrow. I believe the report is true and that on Monday everything will be back to normal, and it's none too soon. I'll write you again tomorrow morning. It is quite late and the mail still hasn't been picked up, so this letter may not leave until tomorrow. Don't be too upset, I know how you feel, but what can we do? Let us hope that things will turn out well in the end. You see, the President does nothing without careful consideration, and doesn't seem easily influenced. Keep on hoping, then.

Until tomorrow, big, big kisses.

Jacques

*Saturday.* The strike terminated this morning. Monday every-thing will be back to normal and our situation will be better. On awakening, I received two letters, one from Pierrette and one from Papa, who informed me that he had telegraphed President Coty (I wonder in what terms!). He received a courteous answer saying that the President had given full attention to his telegram... Poor man, he must have lost his head and asked innumerable questions. Well, I shall have to keep calm now for two months. What a life all the same.

I think I'm going for a walk in a few minutes. It will be twelve days since I have set foot outside, and it will be a pleasure to fill my lungs with oxygen. After that, there will be soup, which will probably be the usual kind. I'm not very hungry, but I feel weak.

Until Monday, then, Mama, and have a good Sunday. Tomorrow I must answer the professor, Papa, Baudet, and several other people. You see I have enough to keep me occupied, only if I know myself, I won't do more than half of the letters. Till Monday, then. I leave you and embrace you with all my heart.

Jacques

*Monday, July 29, 1957*

Dear Mama,

At last this morning everything is back to normal. I'm waiting to go to the canteen to get something to eat, and will be able to relieve my heartburn with some soothing nourishment. And now the time will pass more quickly, which is all to the good.

Yesterday I worked hard. I answered four letters which have been sitting on my table for days. So the morning sped by; I got up late, dawdled, and wrote. The afternoon is not over yet. Due to present circumstances I am reading for the hundredth time my books on minerals. And since recent news from the outside has not been too good, I am a bit anxious.

How much hatred there is all around me! "Woe to lawyers also, for you load men with burdens hard to bear, and you yourselves do not touch the burdens with one of your fingers" (Lk 11:46). History doesn't change much, and those who were formerly called "pharisees" are today called lawyers and so forth. Yet, it is when one is persecuted that one begins to live, and the scorn and suffering one endures here below at the hands of men will be transformed into glory and joy in eternity. "Blessed are you who weep now." In all that has happened, there is certainly a merciful purpose, and what a small thing this life on earth really is! The injustices committed by men and accepted by those who endure them are of inestimable value. There is a solidarity between us all, and if I appear to be stricken adversely by a bitter destiny, this is also a great grace, paradoxical as it may seem. Everything that befalls us is designed to bring about some greater good. The Spirit breathes where He wills, and He gives to those whom He wills knowledge of things hidden from the great.

I assure you I can't help thinking the issue of this appeal for pardon is going to be negative, and I prefer not to cling to too many illusions. For four months I have observed that Baudet, sure of himself in the beginning, has become increasingly anxious. For my part I am waiting for the little event that will precipitate things. There is another similar case which will be judged at the beginning of October, and if my petition has not been presented before then things will go very badly for me, and the press and the public will exult with joy. Well, let's wait and see…

Dear Mama, have a good trip and a pleasant holiday. Rest well. Until tomorrow, I embrace you with all my heart.

Jacques

Monday, July 29, 1957

Dear Mama,

It is quite late, and I am coming to converse with you a little while about some sad and depressing matters! The news is quite bad, and I have just had a conversation with Baudet's collaborator, very realistic and rather decisive. It is actually the first time I have heard her express her point of view as a lawyer, without disguising it in her customary way with useless consolation and illusory hopes. The situation is bad, even desperate. She has given me to understand clearly that at the start we can count on nothing, and that it is on this nothing that we must base the presentation of our arguments, which will always be opposed by considerations of a general order. The day after the verdict, lawyers had already shown her that a refusal of the petition for pardon was more than likely. It would seem now, according to the attitude of the President, that we may still cling to a slight hope. He seems to be open to humane arguments, and will certainly take both sides into account, over and above the need to make an example of this case. Only, only. . . He makes his decision as a man and as the head of the State. After the reception of Baudet at the Elysée, he will preside over the High Judicial Council, and the decision will be debated jointly. It is at this point that various influences will come into play. If he refused to come to a decision at once, it was because he thought the case too serious. And in view of the publicity and the maneuvers of my enemies, this decision could not be taken without due consideration. It will be commented upon, criticized or appreciated, and almost risks setting a precedent. So you see... Obviously, we cannot say as yet that all hope is vain, and there are other similar cases that ended successfully. I did not realize the gravity of my situation before, but now I am convinced of it.

*Tuesday, the 30th.* They say my case will be settled today, and tomorrow or the day after everything will be determined one way or the other. Then there will be a short respite of two months. You're talking about a lifetime.

At noon, I received no news, none yesterday either. Sometimes the mail is a bit delayed. I hope that you arrived safely and that your

holiday has begun pleasantly. Until tomorrow, certainly. Big kisses
and the last page of the story.

Jacques

*Thursday, August 1, 1957*

Dear Mama,

Today at noon I received your two letters from Saint-Germain
and Alençon, but I didn't receive the one you sent to Baudet for me,
and I think I know why. Lawyers' correspondence is special. Their
letters are not opened by the censor, and also a lawyer is forbidden to
transmit letters of a third party or to put them in his client's hands.
Therefore he would not be able to give me this letter through the
ordinary channels. Then too, he must be so disturbed by what he has
just learned that all his attention is focussed on parrying the attack of
the syndicates.

I have in front of me the pile of letters you have written me since
I have been here, and it is impressive. Some people write me from
time to time, but often I sense a painful effort to be charitable, and I
can almost see the pen which has hesitated ten times over a single
word before writing it.

Pierrette has sent me a little note in which she tries to be encouraging, but I feel that she is exhausted and beyond fighting any longer.
Yesterday in the parlor it was quite crowded as three came to see me
together. The visit was a little strained, with efforts at consolation and
the assurance of "very real hopes" which sounded a note as false as
the cawing of a crow. Well, let what must happen, happen.

I just this minute received your little note telling me of your safe
arrival. I am very glad you have good weather and that your holiday
is starting off happily. I enclose a pretty little drawing which I made
during my free time. How do you like it? I have still others to send
you, but I haven't the heart for it after all this notorious bad news.

The chaplain came this morning to celebrate the Mass of St. Peter in Chains, which I thought very appropriate. He too is very reserved with me, but cannot hide his pessimistic feelings beneath his very eloquent silence. A strange future to look forward to! I would still prefer under these conditions to have the appeal presented as soon as possible. The next two months will be truly very painful.

Well, dear Mama, what can we do? But I think perhaps you should begin to accustom yourself to not getting a daily letter any more. I am a little worried about the address you gave me. The Bidou? What's that? There is no house number, no street. Perhaps there's a new postman who doesn't know Madame V. Well, in case things get lost, this is the third letter I've sent you. I'm going to take a little snooze. Have nice dips in the water and good sun baths. Until tomorrow, then. I embrace you with all my heart.

Jacques

*Friday, August 2, 1957*

Dear Mama,

I got up very late this morning after sleeping like a log. I have to admit that I'm beginning to wake up automatically and stare suspiciously at the door, at about 5:00 a.m. Then I go back to sleep for a while until the coffee comes. I hope that by now you have received my letters with the little drawings; if not, they may be stuck forever in some post office or other.

Last evening I received a card from Baudet, rather melancholy and sad. I think the letter I sent him pleased him. He feels a bit lonely in the midst of all those people and the family has not increased his self-confidence with their encouragement. Papa thought fit to write him that all his efforts have been in vain, but that the President had written him a kind note giving him much hope...

The most pleasant moment of my day comes in the evening, at

sunset, when I distribute my bread to the birds. I scarcely eat any
myself, so that I have almost a whole loaf to fill my horn of plenty.
Every evening at least twenty sparrows and a dozen pigeons wait with
wide open beaks until I appear with my treat. They pounce on it like
vandals, and I can observe in each one qualities that are almost human... There is the timid bird who hides behind a stone and gathers
only the crumbs that fall around him. There is the bold one who slips
between the legs of the pigeons to get the choicest morsels. There is
the little thief who snatches from all the others whatever tickles his
fancy, and then there is the fighter who pecks at his companions as
often as he pecks at the bread. Finally, the most touching of all are the
mothers. There are always three of them with their little ones lined up
directly behind them. They come, with a strong sense of their rights
and responsibilities, to select a large piece of bread which they drag
over to their fledglings. And it is adorable to see the tiny birds flapping
their wings to claim their little treat. Each mother puts it into the tiny
beak as if she were giving her little one a kiss. Of course, while she is
performing this task, there is always some bold little character to take
advantage of her concentration to dart up and steal the precious piece
away. And when the mother turns around to peck at her treasure, you
can see written all over her face her stupefaction at its disappearance.
After circling around swiftly, she soon spots the guilty one and flies at
it with a great flapping of wings and unmistakable wrath. After a few
well-directed pecks she recovers her property, and a few seconds later
is dispensing it again. When the session is over at last, I believe each
one has a full stomach, and as the sun sinks they fly off to their nests,
squawking for all they are worth.

Baudet's card shows a cemetery at the top, and below, the church
where he prays every day. I feel that he is much shaken up and morally fatigued... I'll write you again tomorrow as always. Enjoy your
swimming. A thousand thousand big kisses.

Jacques

CHAPTER 8

# SECOND CONVERSION

Beginning in early August, Jacques let the work which grace had been accomplishing recently in his soul, in view of his approaching end, come through in his letters. He expressed his faith in his own wholly personal way. We have said that we were not in full agreement with his way of envisaging "the will of God." But Jacques was a sincere and literal convert. For him, truly "everything was a grace." Obedient in the hands of God to a high degree, he perceived the infinity and delicacy, as well as the exigencies, of the love which he knew had seized him as its prey. He knew his own poverty, which was the very reason for this love. His was the merit of a faithful witness crying out to enlighten the blind, especially those whom he loved, and this with the accents of a prophet.

To his mother-in-law, his confidante, he wrote:

*Saturday, August 3, 1957*

Dear Mama,

Decidedly, you and I are not all that clever. I almost sent this letter to Saint-Germain, by force of habit, and I see that you are sending some very nice letters to your own self. Well, I finally received one of them yesterday at noon. Do not feel too frustrated, nor angry with those who are responsible for this state of affairs. I think there is a purpose in all that has happened, and that we are blind instruments of a Providence which knows only how to build, even if in our eyes its checks seem like disasters.

"You would have no authority over me, if it had not been given to you from on high," Christ said to Pilate. Nothing that happens here below is of great importance really, and only one thing matters to the Lord: to save souls!

Now consider that in order to be saved, one is bound to suffer. "The servant is not greater than the master. If they have persecuted me, they will persecute you also." No one can ever match His innocence, and no one will ever suffer as much as He.

In this temporal life we are led along a narrow path, at the end of which is a little door opening onto true life. In order to pass through that door we must first let ourselves be crucified on the cross which stands at the entrance. If suffering and fear turn us away, we will not enter.

It is true that for the most part our advice is not asked — otherwise how few of the elect would pass through! But with trial comes faith, and with faith, graces, which are not distributed parsimoniously but with profusion. The yoke becomes sweet and the sorrow is turned into joy. What is hidden from the eyes of men becomes luminous for those whom the Lord is drawing. "Do not fear those who can kill the body and who after that can do no more."

Do you know this word of Christ: "I give you thanks, Father, for having revealed these things to little ones and having hidden them from the wise." It is true. All that is despised by the world becomes precious for the Lord's sake. What a troop of lame men, thieves and assassins must surround Him!

A father punishes his child because he loves him. In the same way God, our Father, strikes us because He recognizes us as His children, and He does it for our gain. If we are not chastised, it is because we are not sons of the Lord, but bastards. And who is the Father's heir, if not the son?

Those whom He has predestined, He has also called to suffering, and those whom He has called, He also justifies and glorifies. Understand all the love behind this appearance of evil. "To the eyes of the foolish, he seemed to die…" But it is this death, and nothing else, that gives life, and it is given us only through mercy.

Then too, "may your sadness be turned to joy." Let us not resist the Spirit with our flesh. The Spirit blows where He wills, and gives what He pleases to whomsoever He pleases. At the present time I am aware that He has been given to me abundantly, and I have a firm hope that He will be given to me even more fully.

These are great mysteries we are living through. Do not let us struggle against redemption, under the pressure of egotistical thoughts. The ways are numerous and varied, but the end is one. In the same way a mountain nine thousand feet in height, with a base fifty miles in circumference, has only one summit, yet there are hundreds of ways leading to it. Each one follows his own path and sees only what is within his range. If you climb up the northern side you can't see the southern, but once the top is reached the same panorama stretches out before all.

As for me, I am now at the foot of the highest summit. In about sixty days my ascent will be completed. The present obvious signs should easily convince us of this. "From the fig tree learn its lesson: as soon as its branch becomes tender and puts forth its leaves, you know that summer is near. So also, when you see all these things, you know that He is near, at the very gates" (Mt 24:32-33). *Fiat*, and peace to all.

The mailman passed by but did not stop at my door. Perhaps this evening? I am enclosing a little drawing which has no connection with the contents of this letter but which will perhaps amuse you. Continue to rest well, and do not let yourself get worked up. It is I who have the better part. Until Monday. I embrace you with all my heart.

Jacques

*Monday, August 5, 1957*

Dear Mama,

I feel very tired this morning. It is getting hot again, stifling, and my epistolary enthusiasm is affected. Saturday I didn't receive any letters, so at noon today I shall probably be very rich. Here's a new week, bringing me a little nearer to my goal which is approaching so fast now. I'm not overly excited about it, and I believe that when they suddenly open my door and say, "It will be tomorrow," my only response will be an indifferent "Good enough." It's better that way, provided it lasts!

I imagine you must have had a splendid time and that the swimming and the sea were very pleasant. Did you go fishing? I think Pierrette should go and spend a few days there. It is absolutely necessary for her to have a change of air and different surroundings. As you say, everything will be settled soon enough for her, and it is useless for her to wait in anguish for such a painful day of reckoning, which she can't do anything about. I shall see her on Wednesday and will talk to her about it.

But what will become of her? Her future seems black as coal, and I don't see her climbing back up the slope by her fingernails. Nothing but disaster and ruin. When destiny goes against someone it seems to fly into a rage of persecution which nothing can check, and if Pierrette doesn't have faith, she will be tossed like a straw before the wind, and will be lost forever. Yet I have a firm hope that she will be saved some day, and will be given in profusion all that she lacks now and that she will merit.

But who can say, "I have a right to this"? If I were not convinced that all that happens comes from a tremendous mercy which wills our good, I would be cursing fate and its frustrations. Who is treated with any semblance of justice? Some have everything, others nothing. Those who have everything become blind and let themselves be carried along by the whirlwind of their desires, and those who have nothing end by discovering that they themselves are the rich ones. I think, you see, that we attach too much importance to this life. Its only purpose is to prepare us for the next one, which is of so great importance that in order to save the elect, the worst chastisements await the blessed of the Father.

Understand well that it is not because of what is happening that I have life. The cross which I carry, infamous in men's eyes, is as glorious as that of the monk or the missionary. But how hard it is for those who live in the world to understand all these things. When one lets oneself be carried away by worldly thoughts everything becomes absurd, obscure and so incredible. This is why it is so difficult to save one's soul. I always carry on like a horse harnessed between the shafts, forever trying to break away and dash off into the fields. Yet in spite of himself, they lead him where he does not want to go, because there he will be useful to them. The One who marks out our path is also able to console us, and if to the onlookers everything seems incoherent, light shines for the one who serves as an instrument of Providence.

Courage, then, dear Mama, and confidence. All is peace, all is glory. I will write you again this afternoon, after I have received your letters. I'm going to take a little walk now and eat my soup. Do not be unhappy about me, and make the most of your holidays. Your Zou, who loves you and embraces you with all his heart.

Jacques

*Tuesday, August 6, 1957*

Dear Mama,

This morning I have a cramp in my wrist, not a figurative one but a real one. I don't know what caused it; I had it yesterday too. I think I grip my pen too hard, and am too tense.

At noon I received your two nice letters. You are the only one who writes to me. From time to time I receive a letter from the family or from a compassionate friend, but these are as rare as strawberries in winter.

I'm glad you are taking advantage of the beautiful weather and are getting as tan as a lizard, but you shouldn't indulge such gloomy thoughts. No very simple little black dress, but on the contrary a lovely white dress, and the fatted calf, to celebrate the return of the stray sheep to the fold. Everything should be uplifting. The tragedies of this world take on their full meaning when one looks at life from a realistic point of view. We must be convinced that this earthly miscarriage of justice (and it is that!) is precious in the eyes of the Lord and will be redemptive and bring forth graces in the measure in which it is accepted willingly and offered in reparation. We should not struggle against what has been decided by God. Men are only instruments, and if this seems obscure to those living in the world, it is not so for those who must share in this work of mercy. Certainly, it is not easy, and we must endure a very painful ordeal, but with the trial come graces, and then sadness is turned into joy.

Believe me, Mama, there is no injustice willingly accepted that does not bear fruit a hundredfold, and receive its just reward, prodigal beyond our comprehension. Do not think that all the sorrows that have overwhelmed our family in recent years are useless. On the contrary, they are necessary, in order that just reparation may be made, and that through this the love of Christ may be given us in all its fullness. The law of life is that some pay for others, young branches full of sap are cut back and old, unproductive boughs left in their place. This seems unjust, and it would be, if a compensation far outweighing anything life could offer were not given to these victims, who are by the very fact privileged. Joy, then, not sadness! If life is worth living and if you feel weary and exhausted to the point of death, it is because your soul is famished for the life-giving nourishment which will yield unending joy.

It is only recently that I have come to understand the meaning of the cross. It is at once prodigious and atrocious: prodigious because it gives us life, and atrocious because if we do not accept to be crucified all life is denied us. This is a great mystery, and blessed are the persecuted.

I am waiting for the mailman impatiently; it seems to me he is late today. I am going to receive a letter with very large handwriting which will cover the entire envelope, and which I will recognize from two yards away in spite of my nearsightedness. I thank you with all my heart for the material help you want to give me, and you know very well that I am not bashful, but really I don't need anything, since I am benefiting by a regime that is rather special, and in view of my present position here, anything you might send would only enrich the coffers of the State. So, don't do it! It is very kind of you to want to write to President Coty and I think he will answer you through his secretary, only his "Be assured that we are taking this into consideration…" is not the most positive response you might wish for. But what can we do? There is nothing done that hasn't been done before!

I await Pierrette tomorrow afternoon with impatience. No, she didn't write me, naughty girl. But she must be so tired and depressed that I understand her silence.

Till tomorrow, dear Mama, and take some pleasant walks along the rocks at Bidou, and some refreshing swims in the waves. Do not be upset any more, and chase away the black spiders that trouble you so. I embrace you with all my heart.

Jacques

*Tuesday, August 7, 1957*

Dear Mama,

I feel very tired and have a pain in my left leg. I am going to sleep at noon for a couple of hours before the parlor visit, and then I will write.

I am keeping a little journal, in which I write down everything that happens and all my thoughts. I would like to give it to my daughter later on. She will certainly have many questions in her mind about me, and not having known me she may perhaps have a false idea of all that has happened. And then, even if it is not very interesting, one can get a much truer picture of a person by reading his journal. When you come across an old letter written by a grandmother long since dead, you seem to see her again and can almost touch her through the simple words. On the other hand, the experience I am living through is rich with teachings of all sorts, and the exceptional hours I am passing through may perhaps provide an example. Who knows what life has in store for Veronica? Then too, she might think I didn't love her, and I wouldn't want her to labor under this kind of illusion.

I don't know when this letter will go, since I have no stamps. Perhaps I may be able to get some before noon, if not it will have to wait until tomorrow.

Yesterday I received a letter from Dinant which brought back many memories! It is a beautiful city, with its old houses in the medieval "Kammerzel" (?) architecture of Strasbourg.

Did you visit the chateau of Duguesclin? It is very old but very beautiful. There are quantities of furniture laden with historic memories, notably the bed of someone or other, I can't remember who now. I recall also the skeletons of swordfish with their impressive rows of teeth, and the Hall of the Captains of the Guard. But where are the snows of yesteryear?

Simone also sent me a nice little note, and I am ashamed that I haven't answered it yet. I began to write to her, but didn't finish… I don't know why. Tomorrow without fail, I shall write to "Patricia-Simone."

I hope that you are not too sad and that you're not letting black thoughts invade your soul. Do you know who is the happiest man in all the world? It is the one who, having done good all his life, is killed by men for the good things he has done. A glorious choir of angels accompanies his soul. As for me, I am far from innocent. Indeed, the punishment that strikes me is unjust, but it is precisely in this injustice that the grace given me lies. If I offer up my life I am bearing witness to Christ. A very imperfect witness, to be sure, but one which takes on a precious value in God's eyes. Rejoice in this, that you know I am stricken beyond my deserts. If it were otherwise, you would have to weep, and my fate would be abominable. Do you understand all the love contained in what is going to happen? And how easily it is missed by those who live in the world?

The Spirit blows where He will. To those who must give much, still more is given, in abundance, so that their sorrows may be turned into joy. Everything is a grace. He who first loved us never tires of pouring out all the treasures of His heart upon the blessed of His Father. Have you not read that "the stone which was rejected by the builders has become the cornerstone…"? All those who are scorned by men will be blessed by the Father. "Happy are you who weep now, for you shall laugh." "If you knew the gift of God… ," Jesus said to the Samaritan woman. No, we should not be shedding tears of sorrow, but rather tears of joy, because that which was lost has been found, and there is great joy in heaven.

Dear Mama, until tomorrow. It is very late and I expect the mailman from one minute to the next. I hope this letter goes… I embrace you with all my heart.

Jacques

*Thursday, August 8, 1957*

Dear Mama,

I've had my parlor visit. What an agony! Poor Pierrette is shattered. She does not want to go away for a rest, but wants to stay near me during these coming months. I've never seen her so upset. She suffers for me like a tigress, and above all for her little girl, who is beginning to sense that something is wrong, and cries for me. Poor Veronica, what ravages will these terrible revelations wreak in her little soul? It all seems so confusing and senseless, and our anger flares up because we do not understand. How difficult it is to accept all this ruination!

But look back through the night of time to the long processions

of martyrs, innocents stricken by an unjust fate, thousands of little
children snatched from their mothers' arms in concentration camps to
be tortured. The sky has not fallen, and the blood of these victims no
longer cries for vengeance. Spring has returned and flowers bloom
once more over the graves of the sufferers.

A Japanese soldier wrote to his mother during the last war,
"Mother, I am going to die... If the cherry blossoms flower again my
death will have been in vain..." The cherry blossoms did flower again,
but his death was not in vain.

Of course, you will say to me, does the tigress in her anguish
care what happens to the lion's cubs?

Here the cross appears, in its bloody mystery. All of life revolves around this wood, and if men should be overcome with love
and gratitude at the sight of what appears to them to be life and love,
they ought to be stricken with horror before this image which is only
the projection of their own sufferings.

Don't you have the impression that whatever you may plan to
do with this brief hour that is yours, all of it is marked with the seal of
suffering? There is no escape, there are no more illusions. You know
with certainty that what the world has to offer is as artificial and illusory as the dreams of a little six-year-old girl. You let yourself be
invaded by despair and you try to escape the grief which stalks you
and consumes you, seeking a way out that is nothing other than the
rejection of the cross.

There is no peace, no salvation to be hoped for outside of Christ
crucified! Happy the one who understands this. And the love of God
consists in this, that He "has first loved us" and that once more He will
be the first to lead us to face the reality of our life.

Look at my father. He flees from what he cannot possibly escape. At each blow of the battering ram which strikes him to the earth,
he tries to get up again, stiff with pride. Suffering pursues him, strikes
him, already his cross is prepared, and like a deer chased by the pack,
he tosses his head in one last gesture of defiance.

Do you think all this has happened in vain? Individuality does
not exist. Some bear the sins of others, and the latter are saved by the

former. But who can describe the sufferings of the ones for whom these miseries accumulate? Think of the infinite mercy which directs these tragedies, incomprehensible for those who behold them all over the world. We are saved in spite of ourselves, we are attached by force to the wood, so that we too may have a share in the divine banquet, but woe to him who, in a last thrust of rebellion, rejects his cross!

Concerning the charity of which you spoke in your last letter, listen to what the apostle says: "If I give away all I have, and have not love, I gain nothing. If I deliver my body to be burned, but have not love, I gain nothing. Love is patient and kind, love hopes all things, endures all things…" (1 Cor 13:1-14).

Pierrette needs love — not so much material assistance as understanding. She must be able to draw comfort from a loving heart, consolation for her sufferings, forgiveness of all apparent ingratitude. "Love one another as I have loved you." From the height of His cross, where He was the object of how many revolting outrages, He knew only how to say, "Come to Me, all you who suffer, and I will carry your burdens."

"Do you know what perfect joy is, Brother Leo," St. Francis of Assisi said. "Suppose that when we return to the convent the brother porter does not recognize us and treats us like shameless beggars, strikes us, throws us into the snow and leaves us there, hungry, bruised and shivering. Well, if we have the courage to praise God and to think that this brother has treated us as we deserve, that would be perfect joy." "Amen, I say to you, he who gives in order to be seen by everyone has already received his reward."

Mama dear, until tomorrow. I embrace you with all my heart.

Jacques

*Saturday, August 10, 1957*

Dear Mama,

Forgive me for not having written yesterday, but I had to answer two rather urgent letters and the morning passed like a ray of sunlight in March. This morning I have no more correspondence to take care of, so I have the plenty of time at my disposal.

I received your two last letters describing your travels through Brittany and the way you had to camp out. No, I am not familiar with Mont-Saint-Michel. I understood at once when you were giving me a description of the prison cage of the poor pamphleteer, that your mind was so taken up with the idea of "prison" that you couldn't help being doubly impressed by the misfortunes of this man, which are somewhat mine as well.

Do not be too sad. If you could see things as they are in the absolute your sorrow would be changed into peace. But alas, we are only human and we must suffer up to the end.

Peace, you see, exists in all its fullness, and is never refused to the one who asks for it. It is so luminous that it blinds those who seek it, and they grope in the dark without finding it and decide that this world is really quite poorly constructed.

Mama, it is not that you are misunderstood, but only that you do not understand yourself. You feel a tremendous need to love, and no one responds to this love. Your generous heart would like to pour out the best of yourself upon those you love, and these treasures appear worthless to those who receive them. What could ever satisfy this urge to surpass yourself? Only one Being. And this One is very close to you. He is waiting for you to recognize His face in the faces of all your loved ones, so that He may give Himself to you.

Never write the word "ingratitude." When a person finds his brother ungrateful, it is not his brother's happiness he is seeking, but his own. So many trip over this obstacle. You must give yourself, you must understand that on the day that you achieve total detachment from yourself a torrent of grace will pour into your heart, and joy and peace will be given with an abundance you could never have dreamed of.

There is no salvation outside the cross! Do you understand this? Don't you feel recently as you look around, that there is only a thin veil separating you from the truth, but that the habit of a life lived for pleasure prevents you from piercing that veil?

Mama, the nails that pierced Christ speak less of the world's hatred than of God's love for us. He gave Himself wholly, and still gives Himself to those who do as He did. Tell me, which is harder to do: to give many good things to others so as to see them happy and receive their gratitude (everybody longs for that); or to give a part of your very self, to make a gift of the joy you would like to feel, so as to make others happy at the price of your own suffering? That is what the cross is. Imagine the strength of will you would have to acquire in order to take this decisive step. And how we kick against this goad! All the powers of evil are unleashed in order to prevent us from accomplishing this right-about face. Pride, anger and egoism work together to constitute an insurmountable mountain. And we must climb it, leaving shreds of our flesh all along the way.

There is the cross, and there is our only salvation. All the rest is artificial; it can dazzle us momentarily, but in the end it leads to lassitude, discouragement, and disgust with everything, especially with life itself. Why disgust? Because there is something within us stronger than life, and it is not satisfied.

Everything is mercy, believe me, and I am confident that one day you will understand this more clearly than I, who am coming to the end of my life, and to whom so much is being given — a superabundance of good things and unimaginable joys. "Amen, amen, I say to you, even if I were to silence them, the very stones would cry out for joy."

Forgive this letter, which seems to me rather stiff, and which like the preceding ones is going to stir up a bit of anger in you, like salt on a fresh wound. Remember the Pharisees in the Gospel — they gnashed their teeth… I embrace you with all my heart.

Jacques

St. John of the Cross wrote, "I have said everything in My Word which is My Son. I have nothing more to reveal to you or to answer to you now. Fix your eyes on Him alone, I have placed everything in Him, all words, all revelations. In Him you will find more than you have asked Me for, more than you can desire."

(*Ascent of Mt. Carmel*, St. John of the Cross)

Jacques Fesch followed in the way of this rugged school of identification with Christ in darkness and suffering, even to the point of utter dereliction.

# CHAPTER 9

# PERIOD OF SPIRITUAL NIGHT

*Monday, August 12, 1957*

Dear Mama,

Like the last letter, I'm sending this one to Saint-Germain. I thought that this way your last days in Brittany would not be filled with my moralizing letters!

This morning I feel calmer, but also more alone, seemingly left to myself, which is infinitely more painful. When one moves from a hot phase into a cold one, the latter is all the harder because of the contrast. Joy turns into sadness, and with sadness fear returns. Strength of will and confidence are equal to anything however, and it is in these periods of night that our actions acquire their full value. Sensibility should be mistrusted like the plague, because it leads us into error and makes us confuse our egoism with love. The one who loves, loves in the night, and his love is all the more precious as it proceeds from his will, and then from confidence... This is what we lack the most. We are so mercurial that if we no longer feel, we think we no longer love, and discouragement follows.

No one is tempted beyond his strength, but from each is required some little effort to cooperate with the work being accomplished in us. How hard it is to save ourselves! If only we could realize the value of the hours we live through! Our freedom of choice is precious, and everything is possible to one who believes — everything. The slightest of our prayers has inestimable value. But he who finds himself face to face with reality, after the veil of death has been torn, can no longer choose, and he then sees what he did not see here below, and is judged in the very light of infinite love. Who would not tremble at the thought? Yet how incomprehensible all these things seem, and even foolish, to those who do not see! Faith is a gift. All clear vision comes from on high, and he who looks for answers to his problems in himself finds only darkness and nothingness, and can merely laugh and shrug his shoulders at what he calls "the piety of Saint-Sulpice."

To return to more prosaic subjects, I hope your trip home went well and that you feel a little more relaxed. I didn't like the story of the doggies in the trunk, that must have been very disturbing, especially for you who love dogs so much. Myself, I prefer cats, and I have had a collection of them. They are more discreet and less trouble, and I respect their independence.

Good, I'm impatient for Wednesday to see how Pierrette and our little girl are. Love her well, she is so sweet and innocent. The years of formation she is going through now are so important for her future.

Until tomorrow, and a thousand big kisses.

Jacques

*Wednesday, August 14, 1957*

Dear Mama,

I hope you have taken up your pleasant way of life once more and returned to your house with joy. All should be very tranquil in Saint-Germain at the moment, and with the beautiful sunshine you should enjoy resting in the garden.

This afternoon I shall see Pierrette. I am anxious about her visit because I find her so unhappy and disturbed about the future of her little girl that I myself come near to losing my confidence... I should like so much to console her, but I can't do much. She clings to her sorrow and feeds it still more by ruminations which can only aggravate her wounds. She needs to find peace, for herself and for her little girl, and I am sure that at the end of this long trial which her life is, she will discover the light she is seeking and it will fill her to capacity and beyond. She too is being crucified, and yet she never had anything but good intentions from the beginning. All this seems unfair to our eyes of flesh, and yet if we really wanted to try to see the true splendor of our lives, lit up as they are by the scrap of divinity which dwells in each one of us, all would become love and grace.

I cannot say I have had a very happy life, and if my religious faith were limited to this world I should be the most miserable of men. Yet at the present hour, which is filled with the threat of death, I know that I am the most privileged of men, because what shall be given me is out of all proportion to what is being taken away, and even if I could, I wouldn't change my fate with that of an oil magnate.

These lines must seem strange to you, a little exaggerated, with a kind of contrived exaltation, and I suppose you attach no real value to them, thinking that my imagination is working overtime and that I have succeeded in drugging myself because the hours I am living through are so emotionally charged. You see, there is an insuperable barrier between those drawn by grace and the rest. For the latter, everything seems stupid, useless or sentimental madness, because they see only with their minds or with the vision of their human hearts, and faith is above all that. I understand all this the better because I was an atheist for so long, and sentimentality has never been my strong point.

Do you know my line of thought at present? I say to myself, "What a nasty fright I've had!" And I compare myself to a man who is walking along a road blindfolded. His blindfold is removed when he is ten yards from a sheer precipice. You can imagine him going pale, protesting, and on the verge of a nervous breakdown — then happy and full of gratitude to the one who has enabled him to see where he has been going.

My life span is short, but it is better that way, better that I should die rather than pursue a lengthy road edged perhaps with flowers, but only to end by breaking my bones in some bottomless pit.

Be at peace about Pierrette and Veronica, especially about her whose life in this world risks being compromised. I grieve over this, and it is the hardest thing for me to accept. "Why?" springs to my lips in spite of myself. Yet, I know that the love I bear them is only a pale reflection of Christ's love for them. The future is not ours, and only confidence can save us. They are not abandoned. He cares for them, but with a higher end in view than our mortal eyes can discern. But how can I make this understood? Never can anyone give to another the least grain of wisdom he himself possesses. Could even the genius of a Dante or a Michelangelo enable him to do it? Without the gift of faith a person can see nothing. As St. Paul said, "God has mercy on whom He will have mercy, and shows His mercy to whomsoever He wills to show it. It is not the work of the one who wills, or the one who runs, but of God who shows mercy." And think of the good Curé of Ars, who could not help sobbing each time he spoke of those "cursed by God." Confidence, then, and joy in knowing that that which was lost is found.

Your Zou who leaves you and embraces you with all his heart.

Jacques

*Saturday, August 17, 1957*

Dear Mama,

It has been very cold for two days and I put on my pullover again and my three blankets. You'd think it was All Saints' Day in November. You are lucky. You were able to profit by a beautiful spell of fine weather, and got home just when the rains began. Soon autumn will be here, one more page of life to turn over before the cold of winter. We are both of us old, right? And I am older than you, I am at least sixty! My chariot is quicker than yours and has shot ahead.

Speaking of chariots, I am enclosing a poem of Pushkin, sent me by the professor. It is full of philosophy, and you may think it's not very nice of me to send you such a poem. So much the worse! We should do as the monks do, and always keep a skull in front of us to remind us that all is vanity. We pass away like the summer grass, and where are all our joys, all our desires? Everything passes and everything wearies us, and yet we are above time because we can lift our spirits on high.

This is a strange, unfinished world, where a soul is joined to a bit of matter and cannot live without it. If the soul tries to raise itself, it needs to separate itself from its body, and the body, unable to live without the soul, clings to it with all the energy of instinct.

I received a letter from Papa, who is plunging deeper and deeper into the nothingness of everything. Like an old oak that is half uprooted, he bends with each gust of wind and then straightens up again, clinging to his pride. To the end he will resist, but I have great hope that before he collapses in mortal combat the sap of grace will cause a little green shoot to come forth which may be grafted to heaven and bear abundant fruit. Of course the dead wood will be thrown on the fire, and since there is a great deal of it the fire will burn for a long time, and there will be weeping and gnashing of teeth.

These hardened old sinners are the most frightful. They remain fixed in their hatred and develop an abominable egoism. I am sure that the Antichrist, when he comes, will be at least seventy years old. Well, confidence… I am going for a little walk right now.

I feel rather odd today. At peace, but back to earth. I have a sense of being set at rest for awhile until the sap rises again. It is a continual struggle. When grace draws us, we must persevere on a way of the cross which is not always pleasant, and when we are left to ourselves we groan for this grace which has become as indispensable to us as the air. No more consolation from heaven, none from this world. It is total abandonment. The soul seeks passionately for the one thing it knows it needs: love. And all earthly satisfactions seem gray, stupid and so useless. Well, the battle will soon be over. I shall have been hoisted up in spite of myself, and will be able to go and gambol with the angels and play in the luminous rays of love. Then, when I lean over and look down at the earth, I shall see little devils dancing around you. and I shall bombard them with splinters of stars, to make them fly away…

Dear Mama, while awaiting that happy day, I leave you to go and read my mail. Have a good Sunday and Monday.

A thousand big kisses.

Zou

*Monday, August 19, 1957*

Dear Mama,

Yesterday was a long, monotonous Sunday. I was very tired and didn't know quite what to do. What a life! Saturday at noon I received your last two very nice letters. Don't make too much of this business. The truth is the opposite of what *seems* to be reality. It would take no more than one "hard knock" to leave you upset and turned against the faith. Imagine to yourself that heaven is exactly the opposite of earth, that the more you lower yourself here below, the higher you will rise there, that all that is positive becomes negative, and vice versa. This is the meaning of the scandal of the cross and the foolishness of Christians.

Everything comes in pairs: black and white, night and day, sadness and joy, hatred and love. This world belongs to the realm of hate, and it is lost. Our body is a part of that. Heaven belongs to love, and our soul is a part of that. So there is duality, and opposition between spirit and flesh. One or the other must dominate. If it is the flesh, we will fall heir to the consequence, ruin. If it is the soul, eternal life.

It is not the justice of God that condemns me, but the hatred of the world. I must be stronger than this hatred. I must overcome it by love. And the moment I have conquered my flesh I shall fall heir to the fullness of love. God has only one end in view: to save souls through Christ. In His goodness, He wills to save one who was lost, by giving him the opportunity to take part in this victorious battle. Now, by ourselves we can do nothing; we need the help of grace. Who will receive grace? The one who is content with the world and who commits many sins? In no way. Rather, it will be the one who suffers and is persecuted, because he will cry out to heaven with the necessary humility. How many souls have been saved in concentration camps, on the battlefield and elsewhere? How many atheists have been lifted up, raised to higher things because of circumstances? All that wreaks havoc with the flesh is nothing else but a very merciful grace.

If we lived without constantly offending the Lord we might save ourselves with far less suffering, but because of our sins it takes a very strong remedy to restore us to grace. And if you think some are being chastised for the sake of others, this is because you have a too pronounced idea of individuality. We are all one in Christ. And some are required to make reparation for others because they have enough love to do it. They will receive a magnificent reward, one that only God, who is good and faithful, knows how to give. Everything culminates in the love of Christ — everything…

Dear Mama, I just received a very nice letter from Simone, and another very touching one from a friend of hers. I'm very happy about this. Usually I don't get anything on Mondays.

Good-bye, then, until tomorrow. Have fun with your little Breton pots, and don't scold Pierrette too much for the drawings she stole from you. Till tomorrow, then. I embrace you with all my heart.

Jacques

*Tuesday, August 20, 1957*

Dear Mama,

Things are going worse and worse. The pressure has let up and I am pretty much left to myself, which is not very consoling. You see how hard it is to win heaven; to the very end we are not spared suffering. I must persevere, even and above all in the night. And one day or another, certainly very soon, I shall once more receive the fullness of love, with an even greater intensity, as reward. Really, if all this has to be endured in order to be saved, I wonder what will be the lot of those who live without making the effort. Few will pass through the narrow gate, many will be thrown into the darkness outside.

As to the little drawings, have patience, they will come soon. But I don't know what to do! Well, I'll think about it. I am glad that Veronica will be going on a holiday with her friend... I'm going for a walk... There, the mail was just given out. A letter from the nice young girl in Vesinet. Tomorrow, I shall certainly receive more. I have two or three letters to answer, but I'm waiting for my new ball point pen. Till tomorrow, then. Big, big kisses.

Jacques

*Tuesday, August 21, 1957*

Dear Mama,

It is very late today, so I can only send you a little word, but at least you will have the joy of getting a letter. I have a bad cramp in my right arm and can't write at length. I spent the whole morning trying to write the professor and the result was nothing to boast of. I don't know what's the matter with me. I'm sure I'll be better tomorrow.

This afternoon I shall see Pierrette... I hope she will be in better spirits. Well then, ten thousand big kisses, and I'll write more tomorrow.

Your Zou

*Thursday, August 22, 1957*

Dear Mama,

I am coming to chat with you at greater length today. I have plenty of time and my arm is not paining me at the moment. I feel very tired this morning, worn out physically and morally.

The parlor visit yesterday was not the most comforting. I think of my father! For years, he has despised both God and man, been proud and self-sufficient, and has had only one object in life: pleasure. And since this is no longer possible, well, he is disgusted with life. And it is this attitude he has passed on to three young souls! All this is going to recoil upon his head and is already beginning to. Yet who is the most stricken? What of the sufferings which are going to lay him low… ? Will he even be able to understand them? But all this is useless. Everyone sees things from his own point of view, and other people's experience is never of much use.

In any case, I am beginning to understand the meaning of "purgatory" and I know that all my sufferings are mitigated. Well, I will stop this chatter because you are going to ask me if I didn't swallow a little spider in my sleep that is scurrying around in my brain.

The little drawings are coming. I'm making them, but it is not easy to find something amusing. I want to make some for Veronica too, cats, dogs, and birds, as she is fond of them. I asked Pierrette to send me a lock of my little girl's hair, but I'm still waiting and may have to wait longer yet.

I just came across an old drawing which I never sent you because it didn't turn out very well, but I'll send it just the same. It is of a young black woman walking home in the dark. You will notice the moon and the rabbit. The interpretations you give to the other drawings are alright, but in general I do not tend to imitate La Fontaine. There is no moral to the picture. The point of the story of the young girl and the flower is this: the young man offers her a flower to please her. He is surprised at the effect, and runs to look for a large bouquet in order to receive still more kisses. Well, I'll make up some others. This little one is to help you pass the time. If you look at it against the

light, you'll see that there are beautiful stars in the sky. You see how
I spoil you.

Until tomorrow, Mama. And big, big kisses.

Jacques

*Friday, August 23, 1957*

Dear Mama,

My arm is paining me again and I can't write. Each time I pick
up my pencil my hand gets strained and I get a cramp all the way to
my shoulder. It's useless to massage myself, nothing happens. Then I
rest five minutes after each line, but it's miserable. Yesterday you
were responsible for my earning twenty "francs" since your postage
stamp was never postmarked, so I'm returning the stamp to you in the
hope that you can send it back to me again.

I hope that the little pigs at the fair grounds didn't eat you up,
and that you amused yourself there. It reminds me of Strasbourg and
of Veronica, whom I placed on a little pig on the merry-go-round and
who, each time she came around, delighted us with her beautiful smile.
I should love to be able to take her on trips to the zoo and see her
enjoyment. Alas… I don't think Pierrette is much inclined to this type
of diversion.

When she clings to her grief, she only inflames her wounds, and
the more she does this, the less peace she will find. I know this is not
what she expected of life, nor did I! But we are only placed on this
earth in order to die, and all the goodness of God consists in leading
us toward this act, as consciously as possible. "The Lord gives each of
us our death, that solemn death we bears within ourselves."

Oh, but my arm hurts! Forgive me, I can't write any more. I
hope it will be better tomorrow… I leave you with much regret and
embrace you with all my heart.

Jacques

*Saturday, August 24, 1957*

Dear Mama,

I am sending you the continuation of the adventures of Picre, the little tiger cat who offered you a bouquet for your anniversary. You will notice that he is not as gentle as he seems and that he is a naughty little cat. The next time he will perhaps have become sweeter and more reasonable. I have no other drawings at the moment, except for one other with little birds which is only sketched. I have made the same little cat for Veronica because she is fond of them.

This morning things did not go very well. Boredom with my monotonous life has set in. I am waiting with confidence for the power to transcend these painful hours. That doesn't come from me but from the Lord, who draws whom He will and then allows us to fall apparently, so that we may see what we are capable of by ourselves. It is not pleasant, and my corrupt nature quickly tries to recapture the former state. How hard it is to save our souls! If we knew quite clearly all that would be asked of us, we would give nothing at all, and would be as despicable as before. It is a strange world, which does not belong to us and which we must conquer. Well, perseverance... The battle will soon be over...

Yesterday at noon I received your letter of last Thursday telling me that Pierrette was going to obtain a permit for you! That would be so wonderful! But is it certain? When will she get it?

Baudet returns tomorrow from his holidays and will very likely be here Monday. I'll ask him if it is true. I haven't seen him for six weeks and I wonder what he is going to say to me. He always tries to find out what people are thinking, with a curiosity that is sometimes a bit disconcerting. Well, there isn't much more time left, especially since he will be going to see his mother for eight days, and at the end of September the day of reckoning will be near. How quickly time passes!

I have some beautiful pictures for my little girl, which I shall send her one by one. They are colored and as nice as the rest. They illustrate the Our Father, and show a rosy little girl saying her prayers at the foot of her bed.

I just received your two nice letters. I am glad that you tell me things will not go too badly for Veronica... I hope you are right. The future doesn't belong to us in any sense, and God knows best what is right for us.

As for my father, we must let grace do its work. No one can give him anything. I am certain that he will not die without having understood. . . This depends on Christ, who will give him certitude about heavenly things when He wills. In the meantime, the chalice must be filled up. . . "If the grain of wheat does not die, it remains alone, but if it die it will bring forth much fruit." "All that you ask my Father in my name, He will give you." So, confidence.

Have a good Sunday, dear Mama, and Monday. I leave you and embrace you with all my heart.

                                                    Jacques

# CHAPTER 10

# A NEW SPIRITUAL ASCENT

*Monday, August 26, 1957*

Dear Mama,

Things always go better on Mondays, I don't know why; then they regress little by little. Well, Wednesday is coming, and with it, almost the end of August. After September there will be nothing special to look forward to... so ... and now the days are passing very quickly. I hope the next parlor visit will be more peaceful than the last.

This afternoon I shall see Baudet. I am curious to see what he has to say to me. It is always so unexpected!

The new chaplain[1] came this morning. We spoke together a little while without much profit. Obviously, intermediaries between God and man are useless when the soul has already gone beyond the stage of stammering. On the contrary they become rather injurious, because the point of departure is false and the intermediaries view the paths of others with their own eyes and spirit. I prefer to remain alone...

As to Papa, whom you spoke of so kindly in your last letter, we should not trouble ourselves too much. One day or another, he will discover what he does not yet suspect. Through chastisement, God has us make reparation for our sins, but by the same token He always accompanies the chastisement with the greatest gift He can give us: Himself, His Son Jesus Christ. In other words, the one who is chas-

---

[1] This "new chaplain" was the priest who had come for a few days to take the place of the usual chaplain who was on his vacation.

tised always becomes one of the elect, and this is what will happen to Papa. Others, who live tranquilly, surrounded with honor and esteem, and are never struck by any blow of misfortune, are the ones to be pitied.

I should be so happy if Pierrette too could find peace. There is a sentence in the Gospels which is always appropriate: "Do you not understand that it is necessary that one man die, to save all the others?"

I'm always looking for my little lock of hair! I still have pain in my arm, and cannot continue this letter. I don't know what's the matter. . . ? Big, big kisses, dear Mama, until tomorrow.

Jacques

*Tuesday, August 27, 1957*

Dear Mama,

My arm is still hurting me. It's such a nuisance! I have a sort of cramp from my fingers to my shoulder, and every time I grip my pencil it pains me. Last night, in bed, my right arm, leg and cheek began to be paralyzed. You see I'm in a bad way! If only it were the left side! Oh well, so much the worse. It's just one more trial.

Yesterday I didn't see Baudet. He will probably come this afternoon around four, or else tomorrow.

I am glad Pierrette decided to write me, and I hope she keeps her resolution. I am awaiting the promised note confidently.

I am enclosing another little drawing which was not too successful since it called for pen and ink, but I hope you'll like it just the same — don't look at it too closely! I prefer the last one I sent you. Tomorrow I'll send you some little drawings for Veronica in a letter. These are the promised pictures with notes. I have also made her the little cat on the cowslip, since she is so fond of animals. The little birds will be finished soon, only they need a story to go with them and I prefer them without words. So maybe I won't send them to you.

Did Veronica like the mug you gave her? And when will she be back? I hope Pierrette is planning to go away for a few days with her little girl. That would do her good, much more than staying in Paris where she broods unhappily.

And your permit? Did you get it, or is it still a far off dream? It will be a strange experience for you to come to a prison. But you'll have to hurry, for there will not be many more parlor visits for me — four or five, maybe six at the most.

Papa comes September 4, and with him Nicole certainly. Then he won't come again before October 2. Where will I be? In a short time now, my affairs will be settled. At the moment I feel as if I had years ahead of me. But then, I'm living in another world.

You know, you shouldn't take what I write as egoism. We simply have to realize that life is not what we think. And this is what I should like to make Pierrette understand, for she is still so turned in upon herself. I know very well that she is unhappy, but I almost wish she could come here for a few months to see some truly sad cases, and recognize what real unhappiness is! If you knew all the tragedies, all the injustices in this world! I know that her responsibilities are heavy, but. ... There is only one way, only one! She doesn't want to take it because it doesn't conform completely to her dreams. Nor to mine. I did not want what has happened. I am twenty-seven; I have never been happy, and for almost four years I have been locked up in a cell. And in one more month, it will all be over... This is not what I had dreamed of, not at all... and I shall close with the reply of Sacha Guitry: "One always pities those who remain, but if one asked them to change! ..."

Dear Mama, until tomorrow. I embrace you with all my heart.

Jacques

*Thursday, August 29, 1957*

Dear Mama,

Needless to say, after my epistolary efforts yesterday, my arm is reduced to a pulp. You see, you make me write and write, and I forget myself. Thank you for the news of Veronica. I'm going to send her my little note and the pictures. Thank you, too, for the remedy for rheumatism, but if you think I can buy things in the drugstore... No, they gave me a sort of white ointment which smells like herbal roots and will perhaps do me some good. Anyhow it is fragrant and makes me feel as if I were in a meadow with my nose in the mushrooms.

Yesterday I saw Minette, who was a little more reasonable than usual. I tried to direct her toward a fuller life, more hopeful and peaceful. I should like to see her go back to the circle of people who live with hope, and be able to believe and bring up our little girl in Christian belief and life. She is young, true, and it is normal for her not to live like a recluse... I do not say this for my own sake; I am going soon... But we are bonded together and I have responsibilities toward her. Well, I have confidence.

As a matter of fact, since you want to give me something, there is a little present that I should like very much and it's not expensive — a picture! I would like a beautiful colored picture of the Blessed Virgin which you could send me in a letter. I have none, except for a postcard, which is not very pretty. How would you like that?

Thank you for the photos of Veronica. How pretty she is! Tomorrow her pictures will go off. I am enclosing here a little word for Christiane too. Until tomorrow, then, dear Mama. Big, big kisses.

Zou

*Friday, August 30, 1957*

Dear Mama,

I still have the rheumatism, but it is going away. My arm pains me less, but I have a touch of it in my back, which leaves me somewhat listless. I am sending you a new little drawing which I like very much. Only, my ball point is a bit too broad and I cannot render expressions as I should like to. The baby and the altar boy don't have very nice faces. But he is sweet just the same.

But what is this you are saying! I've sent you many more than ten drawings, not even counting the pictures. You must be confused. This is at least the fourteenth.

I'm almost up to date with my correspondence now, and with this arm it is quite an accomplishment. But I still have to write to Simone and that young girl in Vesinet. This afternoon I'll get to work without fail.

Yesterday I received your letter of Wednesday. If my little girl is returning on September 7, I would rather send her letter to you. That would be wiser. Just now I received a card from Baudet who is making a retreat at the Carmel of Bordigne in la Sarthe. A very nice card! It seems he is mobilizing all the holy monks he knows, and that heaven is hearing the refrain, "Save Jacques Fesch!" And J. Fesch will be saved, and much more. Dear Mama, I'm going to read your letter.

Big kisses from your
Zou

*Saturday, August 31, 1957*

Dear Mama,

I received your Thursday letter, which reveals to me all the anguish you are feeling. I am touched by the confidence you show me, but you know it is often difficult to discern with certitude what remedy one must apply to the errors of others. So many factors need to be taken into account, and in order to make a synthesis, one would need special lights. Obviously, Pierrette is unhappy and in the world's view her future is dark, dry and very depressing. It goes without saying that her cross will always be heavy enough for her slender strength. You see, I think we have to show Pierrette that we love her very sincerely and that her problems are everyone's problems. She needs to feel that she is accompanied, protected and guided with constancy and permanently. But I also believe that we need to make her understand that she must accept the situation as it is. First of all there is the practical point of view. She must have the possibility of making a living without too much anxiety about her own future and that of her little girl. It might be better to get a divorce… But it is a little late now. [Brother Thomas had spoken of a religious marriage, but according to the chaplain this would be impossible and from a practical viewpoint hardly useful.] For my part, I shall do all I possibly can to assure her of a little more comfortable life. But the big thing is this: Pierrette should know why she is alive and what is being asked of her during this earthly life. She needs a goal. She has to change her way of looking at things and can no longer be attached to anything but the one thing necessary. She is young, that is true, and cannot live as a recluse or a nun. That the temptation may at times be too strong… is very understandable, and "let him who is without sin cast the first stone." But she must have a sense of the struggle. It is only a question of orientation, and on the day when she shall have found God, she will be saved.

You know, I don't think we ought to rush her, nor above all give her a sense of insecurity. We should never be too "wise," if we do not wish to drive her away in a day! But no more should we let her take pleasure in her unhappiness. Rather, we need to show her that she is not lost — far from it — but that she has an important role to play in life. I have a firm hope that from now on she will discover what is lacking to her. She will come to it little by little… For the moment, there isn't much you can do, except to be "all love and charity" but not weak.

It is also necessary to let go of all that is past. Let us bury it, and whatever were the faults of X or Y or of events, now we are in the present, which is real and positive, and that is all that matters. Pierrette is a brave girl, and has many fine qualities. With so many friends being concerned about her, I believe she will be well supported, and that you will be able to help her to transform her passivity into activity. She can save herself if she wants to, and she must want to, yes!

Dear Mama, until Monday. Have a good Sunday and do not worry too much.

Your Zou, who embraces you with all his heart

*Monday, September 2, 1957*

Dear Mama,

Yesterday was a long Sunday, and Monday is always a little better. Saturday evening, I finally received the little lock of Veronica's hair with a tiny note from Pierrette. What beautiful hair it is! So fine, so blond, so soft to the touch! I feel as if I had my little girl here with me in my cell, there is a living part of her that I can fondle now. How lucky you are to have her all to yourself and be able to listen to her chatter. Isn't her hair the same color as yours when you were young? There is a touch of gold in it, unknown in our family. I hope she will write me a little note soon and that you will give her her beautiful pictures.

This morning I saw the chaplain, and he seemed a little more hopeful than usual. Strange as this may seem to you, his optimism didn't elate me. I believe I do not want to be released, and the possibility of it leaves me troubled. Right now things are going well. I am ready, and I am living very close to God, so much so that all the world seems dark to me, inimical and of little use to one so absolutely lacking in perseverance. I am too keenly conscious of the truth not to imagine myself separated from Him again, and this would certainly be the case were I to be plunged once more into the wretched and vexatious life that would await me.

Before all else we need to be sure that God's will is being done, but I feel so sure about the outcome... There are signs which do not deceive, and these signs are now being given in abundance. In the event of a [Presidential] pardon, I should be so troubled that I would be in danger of losing my faith... God is good, He always wills the salvation of His children, and nothing that happens ever happens in vain. My individuality does not exist, I am only an instrument of divine mercy. Through me, God would win my father over. He needs above all to be saved.

Our little sister Jacqueline who died at the age of five of diphtheria was herself a sign. At the moment when she breathed forth her soul, she cursed... At five! And immediately afterward, a perfume-burner which was on a table fell to the floor and began to roll around the room. At the same time a picture fell with a crash, and a sheet of glass covering an engraving was extended like a globe and remained like that for a half hour before returning to its normal shape. These signs were striking, but who paid any attention to them?

Now here is the second sign, bloody again! As for me, I am very happy, I am going to find my sister and my mother again. They are praying for me from heaven, and rejoice in what is happening.

Dear Mama, until tomorrow. Give Franklin a big hug for me, it was so kind of him to write me. I leave you and embrace you with all my heart.

Jacques

P.S. I just received your letter with all the beautiful pictures enclosed. There are so many... ! I thank you with all my heart. You have surpassed all my hopes. I'm going to put them up on my wall. Big, big kisses until tomorrow.

Zou

*Tuesday, September 3, 1957*

Dear Mama,

It is earlier today and I have more time to write — if my arm will leave me in peace, that is. Last evening I couldn't hold my pencil and didn't finish my work. I believe it's really a matter of nerves. As they say, a poor workman blames his tools. Well, I am delighted. I have beautiful pictures everywhere. You have spoiled me! There are two that I like especially. The first is the colored one showing the Virgin standing, giving her breast to little Jesus. Her face is splendid for its beauty, purity, and love. The artist really succeeded in painting what he felt. The second is a small one which is very beautiful also. It shows the Virgin again, standing, holding her Son on her left arm. I don't know if you know the one I mean. The legend is, "Holy Virgin, source of love, grant that I may love the Child Jesus like you."

Thank you for the blessing and your personal wishes. The little Jesus will certainly protect me, and in order to prevent me from straying any more, He will bring me back to the sheepfold where there are no wicked wolves. We must understand this, and not rebel against what appears unjust in the eyes of the world. We are only born to die, and it is a great grace to be able to do it in full awareness of the cause, and in preparedness. We must not fool ourselves, Mama, in our interpretation of anything whatsoever. To be admitted to the contemplation of Christ, one must be purified by suffering and must put to death all self-love. Many think this is a priest's tale and that God and the Church are two different things. Alas for them! One day, up above, they will see what it has cost them, to be content with "almost's"!

I received a little note from Veronica. She said: "Come back quickly." Poor little girl! She has a beautiful book about music and seems very pleased with it. I also received a very nice, good-sized photo. Veronica is running or walking in some room, with a big balloon in one hand. She is smiling gaily and looks as if she were having fun. She has lost a front tooth and that gives her a droll smile. Did she get a sugar lump for her lost tooth? Anyhow, Christiane is very good to be concerned about her and lost no time in writing a little letter to my daughter.

And your permit… ! Where is it? Tomorrow I shall see Papa and Nicole. I must speak to him seriously. I wrote to Nicole and asked her to be a bit more serious with Papa. She doesn't understand as yet, and she too suffers the consequences of a negative education.

I've written Papa long letters worthy of the Old Testament prophets. He must be bewildered, but after reflection he will probably end up with an emphatic "Rubbish!" and think that my imagination, stirred up by the thought of the day of reckoning, is working overtime. Who would think anything else? As for you, I'm sure that you do not take absolutely seriously what I write, and that you think it's better this way because at least I am happy.

There can be no compromise in the search for God. The holiest of the saints is still a wretch, full of imperfections. What can we say about the rest of us? I heartily wish people could hear the wailing of a tepid soul coming, all foul and gray, into the light of Christ's glory. It is very difficult to make anyone accept this idea. In order to believe, one must be called, and everyone does not receive the grace at the same time. There are even some who do not receive it at all…

I do hope Pierrette will get moving and make a little effort to face the truth. Personally, I can't do anything for her, she has to live her own life. Until tomorrow, then, dear Mama, I leave you and embrace you with all my heart.

Jacques

*Wednesday, September 4, 1957*

Dear Mama,

What an avalanche! I'm going to set up shop and start selling pictures. I have them all over!

Yesterday I saw Baudet for a long time. We spoke at length of some very beautiful things and he assured me of the daily prayers of many monks. As to my case, we have one chance in a hundred to succeed. Do you understand? You need not imagine that what I write tends toward exaggeration and that I'm getting worked up. There isn't anything much to hope for any longer — really, nothing. I've known this for a long time and you too must be convinced of it. There are many other things I should like to say, but what's the use? All the world makes sport of it, and sees no further than its own nose and the foolish little pleasures that it scatters around in its stingy way. If you knew the seriousness of death and all the sufferings we need to go through in order to approach it in the state of grace!... There's no other valid viewpoint. The nails in the hands are real, and the nails are *accepted*.

You see, I am certainly going through a strange agony and the preparation for this bloody and horrible farce. Well, if I tremble at it, it is not because of physical fear but because I understand better now all the purity of Christ as contrasted with my meanness. In spite of all that is going to happen to me, I shall only be saved by grace, grace alone.

What to say of others? Many have suffered in vain because they did not want to say *fiat* and renounce themselves. Be sure, Mama, that your sufferings are in vain if you do not offer them to God. No one can go to the Father except through Christ, and to Christ, except through the Church. May you finish your days in peace, reconciled with the Church and received into her heart. On high, there is a source of mercy! But one must ask for it, and first put oneself in a position to receive the fullness of grace.

I just this minute received your letter with the photo of Veronica. I send you mine in exchange. It is beautiful, but not like the one you sent me with the doll. That one is my favorite.

I see from your letter that you misunderstood what I wrote you. It is not out of laziness that I want to leave the world. That would be abominable and a sign of condemnation. But it is in order that the Father's will may be done, and because I accept this will with my whole heart I receive joy upon joy. Do you understand better now? We shouldn't pay any attention to our cravings — they are bad and have nothing to do with God. If you have a craving to be done with life, that is a very bad sign, a proof that this world has disappointed you and that heaven is closed to you. To die in such dispositions would be to plunge deep into hell, not seeking God, but yourself. If, when you have been reconciled to God, He should send you a cancer in order to call you to Himself, then your joy would be pure and would have nothing to do with your sufferings; it would be the joy of union, that is all! "Not what I will, Father, but what You will." Beware of egoism. It is not God who is at your service; you are at His.

Dear Mamma, until tomorrow, a thousand big kisses.

Jacques

*Thursday, September 5, 1957*

Dear Mama,

My arm is still paining me — great fun! Well, I won't talk about it any more but will just wait for it to pass. On top of that, I have a headache this morning. I slept poorly. I dreamed that someone wanted to drown me but I saved myself with kicks that had nothing angelic about them. You see what these little devils make me do! In the end they didn't drown me but I can't remember why any more.

Yesterday I saw Papa. We had an excellent parlor visit! He is two inches away from the faith and a mere nothing would send him to the feet of Christ. A little time and the thing will be done. How wonderful are the ways of the Lord! I'm going to write him some more letters to direct his mind to things above, and he will not die without the grace of the Lord. May his example bring light to others and make them reflect a little on the goal of their life.

I am thinking especially of Pierrette, who has grave moral responsibilities. I should like very much to see my little girl say her prayers. Did you receive the little pictures for her? I shall enclose a lizard here, which may interest her.

In yesterday's letter you asked me if I would want to change anything that has happened. No indeed. I have wanted you to understand this: At present, I am living through fragrant hours, certainly the most beautiful of my life; never could I have attained so close a union with God, and without any merit on my part. It is all grace. It goes without saying, a few months from now I might have a relapse, and would suffer much knowing where I had been and where I came from. Much was and is given to me. I could never again say, "Forgive me, I didn't know what I was doing." Judgment would be terrible for me, and I would be so miserable, so weak that in face of the cruel trials awaiting me my strength would give out and God only knows what I might do.

Soon I shall be ready to be plucked like a fragile, simple little flower. Be sure that the Child Jesus, who loves small flowers, will not fail to come and pick this one to put in His bouquet. For the present, the little flower has still to open, grow, and clothe itself in beautiful hues, so as to delight the heavenly Gardener. I await the divine dew without which I would wither, and by dint of asking for it I shall end by receiving it in abundance.

As to my little sister, I think she was taken in order to punish my father for his contempt for God. The signs were convincing enough, and you can be sure that at the present time he is meditating on this subject with horror. You see, it is not necessary to conclude that he is a greater sinner than others. He evidently had many trials at home, but his heart is good, he does not judge and condemn, and this has infinite value in God's eyes. If the Lord strikes him, it is above all in order to save him. God is not a policeman. And if he is saved it is because he has something within him which pleases Christ.

All the elect are crucified — all! If you see a man ending his days surrounded by honor and esteemed by the world, after having denied Christ all his life, you can be quite sure he is condemned. God has pity on all, but the hard of heart, those who use everything to feed their egotistical sensations, those become still more blind, and their hearts become so hard that they see nothing in the end and are damned. Christ has said: "Father, I do not pray for the world, but for those whom You have given Me." That means that the world belongs to the devil and is lost.

If you seek the world, you are seeking the devil, and with him, your own loss. If you belong to God, you seek love and the cross of Christ. Jesus will certainly give you His cross, and this will be the plank of your salvation. If you reject it by an act of despair, you are at the same time rejecting Christ and eternal life. Do you understand? There is no salvation outside of Christ crucified.

Until tomorrow, dear Mama, I leave you and embrace you a thousand times.

Your Zou

*Saturday, September 7, 1957*

Dear Mama,

I seem to have a little less pain in my arm today. I've been able to write a bit more these last days. Yesterday, I didn't get any mail — probably some little delay. It will come today.

Thank you for the photos of Veronica. I like the one taken in the rue d'Alsace very much, she looks like a real little girl. In the other, with her carriage, she looks a bit timid. You know, you have to watch out for that. It's probably a matter of a hereditary glandular imbalance (my own) which certainly could be cured. It could have considerable consequences for her and make her terribly unhappy without your being aware of it. Above all, don't let her retreat into her shell. Let her be open, gay, and communicative. It is a good sign, in keeping with her nature.

I hope that you are managing to sleep better these days and that you do not ruminate on projects worthy of Hamlet. Put yourself in the hands of God and let Him direct your life as He wishes.

As for me, I live always in joy, and in spite of my unworthiness and perfidy Jesus is always near me and draws my soul to Himself in such a way as to cause me to heave ineffable sighs. I'm lucky, right? The endless years stretching before me are filled with sweetness and joy. Who would not want to think a little about heaven? I hope that the light will dawn soon for you and that you will exchange your sorrows for joy.

I have no more news of Pierrette. I sincerely pity her. How far must she journey to find the light? I suppose that she too will have her hour.

I just got your last two letters of Thursday and Friday with the little notes from everybody. It was very kind of them to have thought of me during the picnic. Hug them all for me. As a mother hen hides her little ones under her wings, so you have done with your chicks. May this love draw down upon you the mercy of the Lord, and may He let you see that within your soul a saint is sleeping. I shall ask Him to make you so open and supple that you will be able to understand and do what He wants you to do. Your life is nothing; it is not even your own. Each time you say "I'd like to do this or that," you wound Christ, robbing Him of what is His. You have to put to death everything within you except the desire to love God. This is not at all hard to do. It is enough to have confidence and to thank the little Jesus for all the potentialities He has placed within you. You are called to holiness, like me, like everyone, don't forget.

You have a large ship to steer. You must set about it courageously, but don't count on yourself for alone you can do nothing. It is not you who must act, but Christ in you. And then you will taste the marvels of divine love, prayers filled with honey, ravishing delights and ecstasies, and your soul will climb, without your noticing it, to the summit of love. But for this, you must put self-love to death, and pray. Become the slave of others. Renounce yourself completely. Be like the clay which the divine potter can shape as He wills. The one who abandons himself to God in this way no longer has a heart of flesh in his breast, but a ball of fire. And I assure you that when the Lord begins to kindle the fire of His love, His victim is quick to cry for mercy, for the joy is beyond our human strength to bear. May you, too, penetrate into this world! But don't forget, you have to give *everything*.

Until Monday, with ten thousand big kisses.

Jacques

Dear Mama,

I had a wonderful Sunday, one of the best days of my life, spent in continual joy, light, and warmth. It was the Blessed Virgin who showered me with all this, and she did it in honor of the feast of her birthday which was celebrated yesterday. Who can fail to discover all the beauty and goodness of God in the graces He gives us! It is so good when He touches the soul. Such joy floods it that it can no longer desire anything outside of our Savior. Yes, it is consoling to realize that a sinner like me can receive such gifts. You know my weak nature, spineless, inclining to what is evil and to the line of least resistance. If I am so filled with delights, what can we say about others who are far more willing and generous? May you too turn to the love of God. At this very moment you are fluttering around the light like a blind butterfly. You sense its nearness but you can't make your way toward it because you don't know how. I have firm hope that you too will find it.

You know that I am frank with you, even if it means saying terrible things to you. Well, look — never write and never think that now you have the right to think of yourself a little, and to rest in an artificial and illusory life! If you thought that, you would be insulting the cross.

Mama, after years spent far from the Lord, it is not rest that awaits you, but repentance. You have to expiate and ask forgiveness from God. You do not have great misdeeds to your account, but great lacks. It is this passivity that must be filled up. The acts of love that you are making now, God appreciates and takes into account. Don't think that at present He is saying to Himself, "There's a creature of mine who does beautiful things, so I shall lay up a great reward for her!" Oh, no! but if I may take the liberty to speak for God, He must be thinking that at last you are changing your ways, that your acts of love appease His justice a little, and that as a result He will enlighten you some day, not as a reward but in order that you may realize your extreme misery. Then you will begin to advance toward the highest summits; then you will hate your life, your misery; then saving tears will flow down your cheeks! And the higher you advance, the more abject you will know yourself to be, worthy of all the torments of hell, and the more you will humble yourself in the dust, seeking only the scorn of men.

But to describe to you the joys which will flood your soul — I cannot do it in human words! Do you understand where the truth is? You see, it is the opposite of what you think, and you need a complete conversion.

Look at the saints. Where did they find their joy? In humility, in blows and injury. And the higher God raised them, even working miracles through them, the more miserable they felt themselves to be. How can you say, I have a right to this? God would quickly let you know what you deserve. Try to meditate on the cross a little. You do not understand it. I am sure you do not see the connection between Jesus crucified and yourself. Ask God to enlighten you, and when you come to understand that the nails that pierced Christ's hands and feet have their like awaiting you, then you will be saved!

Alright then, let's come down to earth again. Were you happy to get Veronica back? What a lot of chattering, I suppose! Hug her for me and guard her carefully. As to her future, I don't know what would be best. Of course, England would be ideal, four or five years from now. What I want most of all is to have this little angel brought up in the love of the little Jesus. At six, she ought to know many things! Pierrette should take my little girl to Mass every Sunday.

Finally, dear Mama, until tomorrow, big, big kisses.

Your Zou

Dear Marinette!

I don't know how you'll like my calling you this, and the word "dear" will startle you. You see how naughty I am, using it anyhow. So much the worse. If I've gotten off to a bad start, I'll try to finish better.

I received your note of Saturday and also Pierrette's.

Well, we shall see each other tomorrow. I am very glad you got this permit. Papa won't come, I believe. He is shattered and doesn't know what to think. He will be in Paris at Nicole's house as a matter of fact, but I don't think he will want to return for another visit. Unless, of course, the grace should be given later than we think.

This afternoon I shall certainly see Baudet. We have very interesting talks. I sense that he is overwhelmed, unhappy, groaning under the weight of his responsibilities which seem enormous to him. I try to reassure him on the subject so that he can live in peace, but he is so scrupulous! As if he could have done anything to save me! My destiny has been planned from all eternity and men are only instruments in God's hands. The Lord has made use of His faithful servant Baudet to stimulate my faith, and through this professional defeat He has perhaps wanted to show him how little He esteems this world's glory.

Well, here we are already at the 10th; how fast the time is going! And yet, each day is so rich in God that I feel as if I had lived a year in every twenty-four hours. I am being pressed down and re-shaped. Everything within me that needs to be uprooted is being plucked out. As St. Paul says, "I am in labor — in child-bearing."

You have perhaps been shocked on reading some of my letters, thinking that I am rather extreme. But what would you have me do? In these last moments, it is given me to take into account in a most absolute way the gravity of every one of my actions, and the difficulty of entering through the narrow gate. I say these things to you so that you too may be saved, and that in saving yourself you may in your turn save others. You are rich in the love of God, since He has blessed you with many offspring. Heavy responsibilities weigh upon you.

Much will be asked of you, and without God you can do nothing! So then, have courage and confidence in the love of Jesus.

I'm enclosing a grasshopper for my little pet. The professor sent it to me. Until tomorrow, dear Mama (I've got a sudden pain in my arm just now), and a thousand big kisses.

Jacques

*Wednesday, September 11, 1957*

Dear Mama,

Well, we'll be seeing each other in a few hours! It's a long time since we were together. We've had a beautiful correspondence, but it's not the same thing.

Yesterday I saw Baudet. Always the same thing, nothing new regarding my case. He is looking for last minute expediencies to strengthen his case, but without too many illusions.

Yesterday I received your two good letters which made me very happy. Yes, we must return to the Lord quickly, and never leave Him again. If you could understand just a little of Christ's great love for us, and the gravity of the slightest offense! Well, I hope you will soon be enlightened and that you too will save yourself. You can be sure that Jesus is very happy to see you returning to Him. That was the first thing to do, to make your peace with the Church. And now you must beg the Blessed Virgin to give you her divine Son resting in her arms. Jesus asks for nothing but your heart. He is the One you must love. You understand, we must not make use of God as someone who is to pour out graces on those we love. That would be to prefer the creature to the Creator, and it would offend Him. Do not ask God to save such and such a person, or to help this one or that, but ask Him that you may love Him, and that His will may be done. You must talk with Him familiarly, and explain to Him that you want to love Him well, but that you can't do it, that many things seem obscure and illogical to you, and that you would like to understand them a little better. There you are — pray in this way, put your conscience at peace by a good confession and communion, do nothing against charity (charity of the heart above all, and that is the hardest), ask the Blessed Virgin to help you to recite a few Ave's, and do not hesitate, all day long, to invoke heaven.

I just received your Tuesday letter. Come, come, don't be discouraged. You are all upset over a small matter. Put your confidence in God. Ask Him to help you, and you won't be afraid any more.

I doubt if your children will cause you much grief, but try to understand them and above all to love them in God and for God, and not for your own sake. Christ accepted the ingratitude of men up to His death on the cross... In return, He blessed them! Meditate on that deeply. Without God you can do nothing; with Him, everything becomes possible. So change your sorrows into joys, and the shadows into light.

I'll see you soon. Courage, then. I embrace you with all my heart.

Jacques

P.S. I forgot! Big, big kisses for Veronica's note and the pictures.

*Thursday, September 12, 1957*

Dear Mama,

Now our visit is over. It went so quickly, but I was very happy to see you. This morning I wrote a little note to Pierrette to try to make her understand... I always hope that in the end she will say, "*Fiat.*" Do not be too sad about what I said to you. God's will must be done before all else. Only that brings the peace and joy our hearts hunger for. Dear Mama, I cannot write any more, it is very late and I have that pain in my arm again. May this little note bring you some presence and warmth, if possible.

Until tomorrow, I embrace you with all my heart.

The enclosed flowers are for Veronica.

Jacques

*Friday, September 13, 1957*

Dear Mama,

It is pouring rain in the courtyard where we take our walks and it is gray in my cell, but fortunately not in my heart. It seems there is no walk today. Why, I don't know. That's fine! Are they going to start the strike again? It is so calm in the division!

It is quite early and so I can chat with you at greater length than yesterday. I have come across some thoughts in an anthology which seem made for you, so I can't resist the pleasure of sending them to you.

"Grant that I may say with confidence: Oh my God, forgive me as I forgive others. Grant that I may pray to You with a peaceful heart for those who have hurt me, teach me to conquer myself and to check the impulse which would lead me to take revenge." (St. Augustine)

And again from the same author, "Happy the man who loves You, Oh God, and his friends in You. He alone loses no one who is dear to Him, because He loves them in the One who is never lost." These are two beautiful thoughts which should restore your courage.

You will perhaps think that I have become a bore with my fine lectures and maxims, that I am out of my depth and am reading a lot of things I don't really understand. But you know, I have been in agony for a month. Little by little I leave the earth to draw near heaven, and I see everything from above and with sharper clarity. This is why I can't help crying "Watch out!" when I see others walking a tight rope over a sea of fire. I would like to show them the danger, but they are wearing blindfolds and can't see anything. The truth is so brilliant that it is blinding. Like a butterfly fluttering around a lamp, people whirl around and around it without knowing how to stop. St. Augustine said: "Those who do not know how difficult it is to find the truth may be severe with you, but I, who know from experience what it is, can only feel pity for you, and love."

As for me, I feel that I am about to descend again to a second stage of abandonment which will cause me much suffering. It will be more or less lengthy, and afterwards I shall find grace again in unimaginable fullness. You see the purification which is being required of me. I pass from heat to cold, and the contrast causes me a suffering like the pain of the damned. To know the love of God and not to be able to enjoy it! Well, soon the veil will be torn...

If you like, I will tell Baudet to telephone you in the morning to advise you directly, at about six or seven o'clock, and you can warn Pierrette. The two of you will be stronger together. Tell me if I should do this or not. I have a bad arm again as you can see from my uneven writing, so I will leave you. Until tomorrow, then, I hug you with all my heart.

Jacques

P.S. Here is a butterfly for Veronica.

# CHAPTER 11

# A NEW PERIOD OF SPIRITUAL DARKNESS

*Saturday, September 14, 1957*

Dear Mama,

I slept well last night, because I dreamed of you! You were busy making me some fritters with mayonnaise and in the meantime you sent me out to do some errands. I got lost and didn't get home till ten o'clock at night. I didn't dare ring the doorbell.

Things are much more prosaic today. I have come gently down from heaven, and will be left to myself for awhile to see what I shall do. Then I will climb up again, or rather, grace will lift me up, and I shall be raised even higher than I was before. But first, I must suffer! You see, in these last moments[1] it is being given me to see my whole life and to judge it in the light of Christ. I know what has required expiation and am noting the way I have made reparation. There are actions which I had not thought very serious, but they are costing me dearly. Others, on the contrary, leave me completely at peace. What I should like to make you understand is the suffering we must go through in order to be purified! Many will undergo this purification in the next world, and I am beginning to understand the intensity of the agony endured there. Let us not remain blind! Let us be on the watch!

Since I have come back to earth, I've been thinking a great deal about other problems, especially my little girl's future. "Seek first the kingdom of heaven, and all these things will be given to you over and above."

---

[1] He had only fifteen days to live.

It is very cold this morning; I have closed my window and put on my vest. There seems to be a bitter wind outdoors, and as I am always sitting down, I can't warm up very much.

Yesterday I didn't get any mail. I must say, since I have been scolding everyone like a major prophet, they regard me with a mixture of curiosity and ruffled vanity, and the answers to my letters are spaced further and further apart. No one wants to be treated to "Pharisees, brood of vipers" and other such epithets. The gentle Bishop of Geneva, St. Francis de Sales, always said that one should do everything "with gentleness and sweetness." I'm a long ways from that.

Well Mama dear, until Monday. Have a good Sunday, and don't worry too much. I embrace you with all my heart.

Jacques

*Monday, September 16, 1957*

Dear Mama,

It is very cold this morning and not a wisp of sunlight. Yesterday, during our walk, I was able to bask a little like a lizard, but today I'm going to have to hop around.

Yesterday was a gloomy Sunday. It was the feast of the Seven Sorrows of Our Lady at the foot of Calvary and I meditated on it at length. Saturday, I received your two letters with the prayers. They are very good, especially the "*Fiat voluntas tua.*" Put them into practice and you will see God. I like "Anniversary" less; it is more sentimental, humanly speaking. But the others are good.

As to the photos you sent me, which I studied before reading your letter, I thought I was looking at Leo! How Simone has changed! This is not the little girl who wept for the doggies you drowned, she's now a pin-up girl! You are surrounded by a fine troop of grandchildren. Even so, your family is large and unusual, and I understand how from time to time you long to see them fly off on their own and leave you a little peace! After the role of mother, that of grandmother has been reserved for you, and why not that of great grandmother? It is quite possible! In fourteen or fifteen years, Veronica may perhaps marry, and you still won't be so very old. After all, what would you do without children? You would rest for a month or two, and then, feeling quite lonely, you would look around for some little ones.

Why can't I be outside this prison? I would have so many things to do and perhaps to save or at least to protect! But you see, God has decided otherwise. Once I am in heaven, I shall pray for Veronica until her death, as Mother is doing now for me. Do you see God's design? He made use of me to bring a child into the world, because He wanted to call me to Himself. I am very sure her name is written in the Book of Life.

Very well, Mama dear, I must leave you and write a note to Simone who sent me a nice letter.

Until tomorrow, then, and very tender, big kisses.

Jacques

My dear little girl,

I was very happy to receive your nice little notes, and I hope you will send me some more. I received some lovely pictures of you on your holidays, and I could see what a beautiful little girl you are, and that you were having a good time. I know too that you received a fine writing case so that you could write to your papa, and that you say lots of prayers to little Jesus and the Blessed Virgin. Papa hugs you with all his heart, and he too prays for you, that little Jesus may protect you.

Big, big kisses.
Papa

*Tuesday, September 17, 1957*

Dear Mama,

Things are not going too well today. I dropped gently but surely from heaven to earth, and the divine light is dimmed for me, so that I can see only the chimerical shadows of earth. I must bear up patiently without rebelling, and in a few days I shall be raised higher still. This is what they call being purified by interior trials. I pass back and forth from hot to cold, which is exhausting and painful. You see how much we must suffer in order to go to heaven!

Yesterday I received your letter and Veronica's note. She must be delighted to have such a beautiful writing case. Poor little puss! She doesn't write at all badly for her age. Does she know how to read? And how high can she count? Yes, I don't doubt she is very amused with her uncles. Twelve more days and school will start. Life is beginning to be serious now, and at six one learns many things. May she have the inner strength to rise above the trials which may await her during life. Pierrette has great moral responsibilities in regard to her little girl. She must give her a sense of the things of eternity, not salving her conscience with a little prayer at bedtime but teaching her through stories, talks together, and books.

How quickly time is passing! More than eight days of calm! After that, we must wait for my lawyer to be summoned, and this will perhaps come sooner than we expect. I will of course let you know about it so that you can be prepared. What a bad quarter of an hour I shall spend then! I put all my cares at the feet of the Blessed Virgin, and I am sure that she will help me so that my anguish will be turned into joy.

It is very difficult to get used to the idea. There is something terrifying about passing so swiftly from life to death. I am wondering how the entrance into paradise or the other place is effected? According to the theologians there is a sort of ante-chamber to heaven, where the soul still enjoys a certain freedom of choice before being admitted to judge itself in the divine light. Of course, no one has ever come back to describe it, so we have nothing but suppositions based on visions and the like. But you see — and this is very interesting to note — we pass judgment on ourselves. In other words our sins are shown up in the divine light. We see them with horror, and insofar as we are guilty we absolutely cannot bear to see ourselves in God. This is why it is indispensable to be completely purified at the moment of death. Do you understand why I must suffer, and why, very often, the death of the just is accompanied with these necessary agonies? And then we should remember too that our corruptible flesh will rise on the last day, incorruptible. We will have glorious bodies and will be like the angels! May we all be able to say with Our Lord, "I have finished the work You gave me to do; my Father, glorify Your son."

Dear Mama, until tomorrow, I embrace you with all my heart.

Jacques

P.S. Thank you for Christiane's address. I'm going to write her.

*Wednesday, September 18, 1957*

Dear Mama,

So you are coming to see me again! How nice that is. I shall see both of you wedged into your cage like sardines in a box. I see that you hope I will remain on earth in spirit and that I will not fly too far aloft. Why do you say that I would still have time to merit heaven? You don't understand very well, Mama. Listen to me: everyone in this world has a vocation, a road to follow which is special to him and which is his most direct and sure way to heaven. When we accept to follow this road so many gifts are given us. Some are asked to be religious, others, fathers of families, still others, doctors, lawyers, etc., and martyrs. If the religious wanted to be a martyr, that would not be his way, and no grace would be given him for it. On the other hand, if he remains in his own state of life, he will find peace and joy. As for the one who must sacrifice his life, if he accepts to die, great gifts in keeping with the sacrifice he consents to will be showered upon him. And if he refuses, it will be night for him, whatever he tries to do! Understand, now, that it is impossible that I should be saved in any other way. The sacrifice of my life has been accepted. God is helping me with this, purifying me and taking note of my good will, or rather the absence of all self-will. He is doing great things in me. As for this period of abandonment, you must not conclude that my imagination was working overtime before and that now I have returned to my senses like a respectable person. This is not the first time I have gone through such periods. I can even see them coming in advance. God wants to purify me, and for that purpose He makes me pass from hot to cold in order to make me suffer. Each time that I rediscover grace, I find it in ever greater fullness, and this will continue until I attain a sufficient degree of purity to go straight to heaven. This is what is happening, nothing else.

I liked Veronica's little note so much. I wonder if she has to have her pigtails pulled in order to get her to pick up her pencil and write to her papa. You are right, she is six! ...

Regarding the religious marriage, I'll tell you about it in the parlor. It will be possible, thanks to Father Thomas, and in ideal conditions. *Deo gratias!* Dear Mama, I'll see you soon. I embrace you with all my heart.

Jacques

*Thursday, September 19, 1957*

Dear Mama,

Another parlor visit over. A short half-hour, the shortest of the week! I hate separations. Each time, I say to myself, that's one less.

Also, I'd rather we didn't know too far ahead the day when Baudet will be summoned to the Elysée. I found you calm enough, and rather reassured about the outcome of my petition. Perhaps it's better that way, but I wouldn't want you to experience too great a letdown at the results.

Pierrette seemed a little more peaceful than usual to me, nearer to faith. Confidence... I hope I lisped less this time, but I assure you I never noticed this childish defect before.

This morning I wrote to Brother Thomas about the religious marriage. All the papers are filled out and nothing will prevent its being celebrated. However, I should like very much to have Pierrette think about it with the proper seriousness, and not view it in a sentimental way.

The professor wrote me and sent some photos of himself and his wife. They are both very nice. But he is a Marxist socialist, more or less an atheist, and my ponderous Christian tirades weary him beyond description. I even feel that he is troubled, and is asking himself, "Who is this gadfly stinging me?" I prefer Father Thomas' letters. He knows how to read between the lines and immediately understands the state of a soul. He sees God through the Christian. I am very glad to have this holy monk praying for me.

Mama dear, until tomorrow, I hug you with all my heart.

Jacques

# CHAPTER 12

# NEARING THE END:
# NEW AND FINAL SPIRITUAL ASCENT

*Friday, September 20, 1957*

Dear Mama,

Well, the end is approaching, and what you have blindly refused to admit will soon be upon me. Five more days to live, perhaps ten at the most. My lawyer will be summoned any day now to present the petition for pardon. I have asked him to let you know on the morning of the day, and he will phone you or have someone else phone you. I prefer that Pierrette should know nothing in advance, and I want you to be the first to tell her. They will notify you around six in the morning and I will write you which are the days to watch out for, but at the moment I don't know anything myself. I don't want Pierrette to learn it in the newspapers or on the radio, so I entrust you with this painful duty.

I hope that my recent letters have helped you a bit to see things from a different point of view than the strictly human one. Above all I have wanted to make you understand the cross. Crucified love! Was there ever a greater crime? It is this sacrifice which saves us, and it is through it that Jesus continues to live here below. Understand, then, that my death is but a poor enough repetition of Calvary. It is unjust, inhuman and barbaric. I accept it as such and offer it for those whom the Lord wants to save. It is a great sacrifice, and the blood which will flow, seemingly in vain, will in fact be regenerative.

You must keep your promise to me to accept this death, otherwise I will not go in peace. You must prepare yourself by prayer for all that will happen, and offer everything to God instead of making your grief the center of the world. Let Pierrette go to confession and Holy Communion. In a few days, she will have need of this. Papa wrote me, but he is as undiscerning as you. "Sleep soundly," you say!

Until tomorrow, Mama dear, and do not worry too much about me. Since this morning, I have mounted to heaven, and will again be living in Paradise. I embrace you with all my heart (with painful arms). Thank you for the little doves and the photo, and extra big kisses from your tall son.

                                                    Jacques

*Monday, September 23, 1957*

Dear Mama,

Well, tomorrow my fate will be determined, or rather, tomorrow the final decision will be made, and a few days from then I shall enter into blissful eternity "where all fear is banished." I hope you are beginning to open your eyes and that you will no longer refuse to admit the inevitable; otherwise you will take a bad tumble and make yourself very ill. I should have liked to leave Pierrette spiritually armed for the trials she has yet to go through. Only, you know her better than I, or at least as well. Above all, don't see divine injustice in what happens. It is earthly injustice, but from that point of view nothing is very important. Do not forget that it is not God who is at your service, but you at His. God is not an automatic distributor of temporal benefits to sinners who have come upon hard times. He loves men, and has only one object: to give Himself to them for all eternity, not to give them a pleasant life on earth which will generate sins, and then bring souls who have injured Him to Paradise! If you understand that this life is nothing, you will not have lost me, and you will live in joy in the measure in which you renounce yourself.

Do not worry too much about Veronica and the consequences of this tragedy on her future. We must trust God. No one knows what tomorrow will bring! We must give her the one good which no one can ever take from her. God will help you in the measure in which you trust Him. But we are so constructed that we depend first on ourselves, and only afterwards on God...

As for me, I am at peace, and so far have managed not to be the least bit upset. It seems to me that what is going to happen is the most natural thing in the world. You see the goodness of God, who not only promises me an eternity of happiness, in spite of all my sins, but even carries me there in an armchair, with all the gentleness and goodness of a father who loves his children!

Thank you for the photos. I don't recognize Veronica any more — she changes from day to day. But I like these pictures a little less than the ones of a few months ago. She is growing into an awkward stage and it's hard to tell whether she's a caterpillar or a butterfly. In any case, she's tall, very slight, very slender. The children have changed a lot too. I don't know Patrick from Franklin, Philip looks as if he didn't want his picture taken, and Simone has become a young lady. Veronica has your family's smile. I recognize it in all the children. Well, she must be having fun at home, and it's a good thing you have kept her with you. Otherwise, where would she go? "Whatever you do for the least of these little ones, you do it for Me."

My arm is paining me again. Until tomorrow, Mama dear, I embrace you with all my heart.

Jacques

*Monday, September 23, 1957*

Dear Mama,

Thank you for your message this evening which helped me so much. May you keep these good dispositions all your life! Yes, it is on that level that you must view your existence, "for if they do these things in the green wood, what shall become of the dry?"

This execution which frightens you is nothing in comparison with what awaits sinners in the next world! It is not for me that you should weep, but for sins which offend God. As for me, I am happy. Jesus is calling me to Himself, and great graces have been given me. If you could only taste for a single instant the sweetness of the transports of divine love! And could realize the absolute gravity of the slightest offense! God must come first, do not forget it. He calls you and believes in you. You are rich in His love. Many souls are linked with yours, and you will have an account to render.

You must go to Christ, without whom you can do nothing. If you seek Him, you will find Him, but you must seek Him with all your heart. I'm always afraid that without realizing it you are seeking yourself rather than God. You are the handmaid of the Lord, therefore you owe Him complete submission. The Lord is your inheritance, therefore you owe Him thanks.

Above all, do not seek your own will, but His. Shut out all other thoughts; do not argue. Make your peace with the Church and pray regularly, that is, a certain number of prayers to be recited daily (especially the rosary). Go to Mass on Sundays and communicate as often as you can. If you do this conscientiously, I promise you that one day when you least expect it grace will flood your soul and you will cry out, "How wonderful!"

Do not use intermediaries to go to God. It is not Veronica who will bring you to God, but you who should approach Veronica through God. Your adoration should go to God directly, and the love with which He will fill you, you will then give to Veronica.

Mama, guard your heart! God wants you to love Him for Himself, by an act of your will, and not for the sweetness which He pours into the souls of those who please Him. Otherwise, it is not God you are loving, but yourself. Read many spiritual books, too — the Gospel and Epistles, the life of Jesus (*Jesus and His Times*, Daniel-Rops), and the lives of saints — and you will see a wonderful world unfolding before your eyes!

*Tuesday, the 24th.* Today the President will receive my lawyer, at about 11:30. This afternoon, I will have the report of the meeting, although when all is said and done there won't be anything of much interest to learn. It seems that Pierrette too is crushed! I tried to warn her, but no, she wouldn't believe anything I said. It is high time she turns to God, instead of cultivating her grief as she is doing. She worries about her little girl's future, as if she were capable of changing anything by herself! I hope that Father Thomas will spend some time with her these days, and direct her tears to a better object.

I am also happy to see Papa and to note the progress of grace in his soul. But they're all wearing such blinders! It is good that Veronica was admitted to that religious boarding school. They will bring her up well there, giving her moral and religious balance. The education of the little ones is so important. Whatever happens, she will never lose the fruit of these young and innocent years.

Dear Mama, until tomorrow, I leave you, and embrace you with all my heart.

*Wednesday, September 25, 1957*

Dear Mama,

I can only send you this little note today. It is very late, and my arm is paining me. You realize, I'm sure, that in these last days I have piles of letters to write, and as I can't write quickly I'm trying to get a head start. Tomorrow, I'll write you more at length. Stay calm and peaceful. Put all your confidence in God, and pray. My heart is joyous, and heaven is beginning to descend into my soul. I embrace you with all my heart.

Jacques

*Thursday, September 26, 1957*

Dear Mama,

Things aren't going so well today. I have a sick stomach, which is upsetting, and a headache, and as a result my sweet peace is a bit affected. I'm going to take something soothing right now, and I hope I'll feel better. You know how it is, when one member suffers, all the rest suffer with it. In these last moments I need to have my body functioning smoothly, in order to be at peace.

Yesterday, I really couldn't see you in the parlor. Papa was zooming around like a meteor, he felt so ill at ease, and Monica was following him. Pierrette was calmer, more confident, closer to God. I thank Father Thomas for this; his presence is really a help in these last moments. I'm going to see him this afternoon. Provided that I'm better than this morning, for I'm feeling rather green at the gills!... Plus, I'm cold.

I can well imagine that you are spending sleepless nights, and that your days are filled with anguish, sorrow and pain. What can we do? There is only One who can heal these wounds. Ask Him to do it. Be very sure that God, in His divine providence, has foreseen this grief which overwhelms you today, and which may perhaps compel you to draw a little closer to Him. Ponder this carefully. What you see here is only a pale reflection of what will take place in the next world — and executions are utterly horrible. Act in such a way as to be at peace yourself, and do not forget how much suffering is needed to be worthy of our Lord Jesus Christ!

Take good care of my little girl, so that she will grow up well-balanced and loving God, bringing forth the good fruit of a good tree destined to be transplanted one day in Paradise. Dear Mama, I have such a pain in my heart that I'm going to lie down on my bed for a little while... I'll finish this later. Big, big kisses... .

... I'm not feeling any better, so I'll have to leave you for today. I still have that pain.

I embrace you with all my heart.

                                                    Jacques

*Friday, September 27, 1957*

Dear Mama,

I'm better today. My nausea is beginning to lessen but I certainly felt wretched with it. I'm going to take a little nitrate of bismuth this morning. I am always at peace, and confident.

Yesterday I saw [Father] Thomas, and I think we must have had an angel sitting there with us, there was so much peace and joy in that holy conversation. Perhaps I'll see him again next Monday or Tuesday — if it's possible, of course. I am content that the Lord permitted him to come and concern himself with my affairs with such eager love. It is thanks to him that all can be arranged so happily!

What he told me of Pierrette made me tremendously happy. She has already received great graces, he assured me, and he is going to concern himself about her and my little girl with all his customary zeal and devotedness. Oh, that you, too, might enter into this circle of peace around which you have been fluttering for so long. You are all ready to enter into it — a mere nothing stops you; but you yourself create the obstacle, because you still don't want to renounce yourself. It is not impulsiveness that holds you back. If you do what I told you, you will be saved; if not… it will be you who reject Christ, and I very much fear that you will have to endure some bitter consequences! Of course, everyone can't be converted overnight; the work of grace is sometimes slow. Perhaps Jesus wants you to come to Him initially through the charity you show to those who depend on you. When He shall have noted the purity of your heart and the nobility of your intentions, then perhaps He will make Himself known to you. I hope for this with all my heart! There is no salvation outside of Jesus crucified!

I received your pretty pictures and your Wednesday letter. Yes, I can imagine the chagrin you felt at having to stay outside. Poor Mama! But what can we do, we have to resign ourselves to events, and I am happy to see that you do. Remain calm above all, and submissive. Think of the Blessed Virgin, who remained for hours beneath the cross without rebelling! It is to her that you must entrust yourself. If God permits it, I will pray for all of you from heaven. There is a communion of souls, but for that we must be in the necessary state. You can do nothing without God and God can do nothing without you. There is only one thing stronger than love, and that is the refusal of love!

Dear Mama, I don't know if tomorrow... well, I won't think about it. I'll write you a good-bye letter in any case. I embrace you with all my heart.

Jacques

*Saturday, September 28, 1957*

Dear Mama,

Here I am feeling wretched again today. I have a pain in my leg, which puts me into a sorry mood in these final moments of mine. So I can't write you at any length. My spirits are steadily good, at least when my leg leaves me a little peace, and I have had some delightful hours, with my head in heaven, far from all anguish.

Yesterday I had an excellent day, except towards evening when I began to shiver with cold. I went to bed, but woke up this morning with an upset stomach. I am waiting for some soothing medication, and am going to try to eat a bit more regularly.

Last evening I saw my lawyer for a brief hour. Enough said... Now we've come to Saturday! Today I shall perhaps see his partner, although she has a horror of coming to a place like this! Tomorrow, I shall see no one, and Monday, probably Father Thomas and perhaps Baudet also in the evening. Although from the moment when the charge is "officially" announced, he cannot stir from his home.

Anyhow, confidence in God is all I need. No harm will come to me, and I shall be carried straight to paradise with all the gentleness

lavished on a new-born babe. I hope that this evidence of God's goodness and the power of grace will bring you to see how profitable it is
to draw near to the Lord without fuss or reservations. Tell yourself
that I am being struck by love, not chastisement! The execution of the
damned in the next world is far more terrible than what frightens you
so much now. Weep for yourself, for your sins, and fear a just retribu-
tion for your iniquities. Only, as Christ Himself said, even if a dead
man were to return to the living, still they would not believe. This is
a blind and evil generation! If only I could open the eyes of all men ...
alas!

Well, Mama dear, until Monday. Pray a little with Pierrette too.
You will perhaps find peace in doing that. I leave you and embrace
you with all my heart.

Jacques

THE LAST LETTER[1]

*September 30, 1957*

Dear Mama,

We have been writing so often to each other in the last six months
that in this final letter I can only urge you to persevere in the way you
are going, in which you have just made a little progress, for now you
know the way. Try to open your eyes wide and to discern, behind
what seems like chastisement, the manifestation of the divine will,
which is love. Do not turn in on your grief. Take it to God, and let only
one thing cause you to suffer: offenses committed against Him. This,
you see, is the great goal of life. We are all mortal, and must leave this
valley of tears sooner or later. The essential thing is to leave it in a
good state of soul.

Be confident about me. God has given me the great grace of

---

[1] Jacques also wrote other farewell letters, to his wife and other persons dear to him. They
have not yet been published.

drawing me to Himself, and when you read these lines I shall be looking upon our Lord Jesus Christ. I confess that I am a little fearful of your impulsive reactions, dictated by your profound grief. Above all, remain calm; be moderate in everything, and try to plunge your sorrow in the love of Jesus, who waits only for your appeal to come and console you. Leave all justice, all vengeance, in God's hands: this is my formal will. Christ came to save the world, not to condemn it. Let us not condemn ourselves, even if others do so. Seek peace. You have, if you are willing, a great and beautiful role to fill. Many depend upon you, much will be asked of you, but by the same token, much will also be given you provided you do not resist.

I hope with all my heart that in time you will be reconciled with our Holy Mother Church. It is she who distributes all of Christ's gifts. In rejecting her, you deprive yourself of all the helps, benefits and graces which Christ has placed within her. Think this over.

Dear Mama, first of all I want to thank you deeply for all the love with which you have surrounded me during these last months. I am looking at the pile of your letters, which have strengthened me. Each one has been the center of every day for me, and without them I should have suffered deeply. You know what Jesus said in His Gospel: "I was in prison and you visited me... ." In surrounding your child with love, it is also Christ you have comforted, and I am very sure that He will reward you. Don't forget that charity covers a multitude of sins! If many things seem dry or incomprehensible to you, you can rise above them through charity. Charity is kind and patient, it believes all, hopes all, never ends. Don't forget that God is love!

With these lines, I entrust my little girl to you. Take good care of her, with love and serenity. Think that Jesus loves her infinitely and that what you do for one of these little ones, you do for Him. Love her in God and be sure that from heaven I will protect her and watch over her with all the love Jesus will give me. Abide, you too, in the love of Christ, and you will see God.

Now, my life is finished. "Like a little spring flower which the divine Gardener plucks for His pleasure," so my head will fall — glorious ignominy — with heaven for its prize! I am happy...

Good-bye, dear Mama, and may the Lord keep you, you and all yours.

I embrace you in Christ and Mary.

> Your son in God,
> Jacques

Jacques did not forget his friend, the other prisoner, and gave the chaplain this poem for him:

To my friend Robert, with the hope that he too will rejoice in the dawn!

> He said, it is good to part in the night
> Toward the end of exile, toward the shining dawn
> He whose soul here below was covered in veils.
> Then forth he went to the sound of sobs
> Forth to the black scaffold and the bloody block
> Eyes open, eager, upon the stars.
> Until we meet in God.

> Your brother Jacques

Had not Jacques written to Brother Thomas on his last night, "I wait in the night and in peace... I wait for Love"?

# TESTIMONIAL

Letter of the chaplain of la Santé to Father Thomas, written shortly after Jacques' death.

*Paris, December 8, 1957*

My very dear Father,

I did not write you after Jacques' death, thinking that you would have already been apprised of his last moments. You know what his sentiments were before his execution. Jacques had been as closely united to Our Lord as it is possible to be. His spiritual ascent became an absolute fact from the moment when, last August, he became detached from all that is human, in order to attach himself to Our Lord, and when he accepted his sacrifice. From that moment on, he told me himself, the outpouring of grace had been extraordinary. I had always feared a kind of cynicism in him, a certain fatalistic acceptance. He showed this at the time of his mother's death.[1] I wondered if this cynicism was going to reappear, at least exteriorly, at the moment of his execution. Thanks be to God, there was no sign of it.

On Monday evening, September 30, knowing that he would be guillotined the following morning, Jacques went to bed, slept, awoke during the night (the guard on duty gave me this information) and asked what time it was.

---

[1] The prison chaplain, not understanding Jacque Fesch's reserved nature, mistook his attitude for cynicism. Although he did not show his pain outwardly, Jacques Fesch was very much affected by his mother's death. See in *Light Over the Scaffold*, the first part of this book, his letter of June 8, 1956 to Brother Thomas and those of January 31, April 11, May 17 and 30, 1956, in which he showed great concern for his mother's moral and physical welfare.

"Three o'clock in the morning."

He then asked for a light, "because I have to get ready at once." He got up, made his bed, and took up his missal. This is how I found him on entering his cell at 5:30. Jacques was very courageous. He was afraid he wouldn't be able to "sustain the shock" physically,[2] so he did all he could to see that everything would proceed as quickly as possible. I heard his confession for the last time. His communion, which followed, was very moving. I spoke briefly with him. His answers were calm, his peace profound. Then he fell silent. I faced him when they bound his hands, so that I might comfort him. The executioners had him mount the scaffold. At once, Jacques said to me, "The crucifix, Father, the crucifix," and kissed it many times. These were his last words. It was very moving and those present were deeply touched. Jacques had offered his life for the conversion of his father, for those whom he loved, and for the man he had killed. There was not the slightest note of rancor, or even of bitterness, in his attitude. He died a great Christian.

This, dear Father, is what Jacques was. You contributed much to the preparation of his soul. As he promised me on the eve of his execution, he is praying for us now. I am convinced of it.

Very fraternally yours,
Father Devoyod, OP

---

[2] Jacques had refused the traditional glass of rum and the cigarette offered to the condemned at the moment of their execution.